T0078091

Spirit to Spirit

DON LITTON

authorHOUSE

AuthorHouse™
1663 Liberty Drive
Bloomington, IN 47403
www.authorhouse.com
Phone: 833-262-8899

Published by AuthorHouse 10/25/2021

ISBN: 978-1-6655-4188-6 (sc)
ISBN: 978-1-6655-4187-9 (e)

Print information available on the last page.

Any people depicted in stock imagery provided by Getty Images are models, and such images are being used for illustrative purposes only. Certain stock imagery © Getty Images.

Scripture quotations marked NASB are taken from the New American Standard Bible®, Copyright © 1960, 1962, 1963, 1968, 1971, 1972, 1973, 1975, 1977, 1995 by The Lockman Foundation. Used by permission.

Scripture quotations marked NIV are taken from the Holy Bible, New International Version®. NIV®. Copyright © 1973, 1978, 1984 by International Bible Society. Used by permission of Zondervan. All rights reserved. [Biblica]

Scripture quotations marked NLT are taken from the Holy Bible, New Living Translation, copyright © 1996, 2004, 2007. Used by permission of Tyndale House Publishers, Inc. Carol Stream, Illinois 60188. All rights reserved. Website

Scripture quotations marked RSV are taken from the Revised Standard Version of the Bible, copyright © 1946, 1952, 1971 by the Division of Christian Education of the National Council of the Churches of Christ in the USA. Used by permission.

Scripture quotations marked KJV are from the Holy Bible, King James Version (Authorized Version). First published in 1611. Quoted from the KJV Classic Reference Bible, Copyright © 1983 by The Zondervan Corporation.

This book is printed on acid-free paper.

Contents

Acknowledgment vii

Introduction ix

Chapter 1:   "In the beginning" - "God" 1

Chapter 2:   Kindred Spirits 11

Chapter 3:   David and Jonathan 19

Chapter 4:   Naomi and Ruth 35

Chapter 5:   Elijah and Elisha 41

Chapter 6:   Moses and Aaron 53

Chapter 7:   Spirit to Spirit 67

Chapter 8:   Testing the Spirits 77

Chapter 9:   He Touched Me 83

Chapter 10: Worship Him in Spirit 87

References 95

Appendix 1 97

Appendix 2 99

Acknowledgment

Writing a book was harder than I thought and more rewarding than I could have ever imagined. No one in life does anything worthwhile alone. I would not have made it this far in my book had not my sister, Rita Litton Ellis, spending countless hours reading, correcting, and revising sentences and paragraphs of my manuscript and for that, I say, "THANK YOU"!

My calling represents a specific set of tasks to be carried out in the world. This represents my life's work and cannot be born of your ideas for it to have any meaning. As I began to write about Biblical subjects and my spiritual experiences, I felt my knowledge was limited in SCOPE. I know I came into this world with a purpose and at a certain stage in my development, my calling in life began to emerge. Before this happened, I built in my mind great ideas about who we are in the world, what the world must be, what you and I must be, what I will do, what you and I and others should do and so forth.

Alone we have no real purpose, meaning or direction; we have no real identity alone. However, as an individual expressing my need of God, I began to have purpose, meaning and direction as I walked with God. When my experience of higher purpose matured to a certain point, my calling emerged. God's Plan is established for our success. With that said, my missionary endeavors and pastoral efforts came into being and now all of that is a fleeting memory for this senior pilgrim. More importantly, I thank God for the journey, age 76, and to have KNOWN HIM for 58 years. Being a "Born Again" Christian, the Lord has guided me with HIS eye and it has been an insane walk with HIM. Only a foolish man would say I know a lot about God because in my case the more I have learned about HIM, the less I realize I know.

So now for the final leg of my journey, I am writing about HIM (lol). Thanks for reading this book and I cannot apologize for using so much SCRIPTURE; it's what I know as my SOURCE.

Introduction

What is the spirit world? The Bible teaches that an unseen world of spirits surrounds us. It is both real and powerful. While various people, some with and some without God's consent, may actively engage this invisible world. In the beginning:

> **Genesis 1:1-2** - "God created the heavens and the earth. The earth was without form, and void; and darkness was on the face of the deep. And the Spirit of God was hovering over the face of the waters" **(KJV)**.

Among the Israelites, the penalty for anyone practicing spiritism was death.

> **Leviticus 20:27** - "A man or woman who is a medium or a spiritist among you must be put to death" **(NIV)**.

Spiritist philosophy says that humans, along with all other living beings, are essentially immortal spirits that temporarily inhabit physical bodies for several necessary incarnations to attain moral and intellectual improvement. It also asserts that spirits, through passive or active mediumship, may have beneficent or malevolent influence on the physical world. Spiritism is an evolution-affirming religion. God tells us in:

> **Isaiah 8:19** - "And when they say to you, 'Seek those who are mediums and wizards, who whisper and mutter,' should not a people seek their God" **(KJV)**?

Spiritists and mediums were common among the pagan peoples of the Bible lands. God warned the children of Israel against becoming involved in these practices just prior to their entry into the Promised Land of Canaan.

Deuteronomy 18:9 - "When you enter the land the Lord your God is giving you, do not learn to imitate the detestable ways of the nations there. Let no one be found among you who sacrifices his son or daughter in the fire, who practices divination or sorcery, interprets omens, engages in witchcraft, or casts spells, or who is a medium or spiritist or who consults the dead. Anyone who does these things is detestable to the Lord" **(NIV)**.

The Bible strongly condemns spiritism, mediums, the occult, and psychics:

Deuteronomy 18:10-13 - "Let no one be found among you who sacrifices their son or daughter in the fire, who practices divination or sorcery, interprets omens, engages in witchcraft, or casts spells, or who is a medium or spiritist or who consults the dead. Anyone who does these things is detestable to the LORD; because of these same detestable practices the LORD your God will drive out those nations before you. You must be blameless before the LORD your God" **(NIV)**.

Horoscopes, tarot cards, astrology, fortune tellers, palm readings, and seances fall into this category as well. These practices are based on the concept that there are gods, spirits, or deceased loved ones that can give advice and guidance. These "gods" or "spirits" are demons:

II Corinthians 11:14-15 - "And no wonder, for Satan himself masquerades as an angel of light. It is not surprising, then, if his servants also masquerade as servants of righteousness. Their end will be what their actions deserve" **(NIV)**.

The Bible does not give us any reason to believe that deceased loved ones can contact us. If they were believers, they are in heaven enjoying the most wonderful place imaginable in fellowship with a loving God. If they were not believers, they are in hell, suffering the unending torment for rejecting God's love and rebelling against Him.

> **Leviticus 20:6** - "I will set my face against the person who turns to mediums and spiritists to prostitute himself by following them. I will cut him off from his people" **(NIV)**.

The end result of King Saul's quest was tragic. Shortly after his visit to the witch, the king was wounded in battle and took his own life rather than being captured by the enemy.

Satan pretends to be kind and helpful. He tries to appear as something good. Satan and his demons will give psychic information about a person in order to get that person hooked into spiritism, something that God forbids. It appears innocent at first, but soon people can find themselves addicted to psychics and unwittingly allow Satan to control and destroy their lives. Peter proclaimed:

> **I Peter 5:8** - "Be alert and of sober mind. Your enemy the devil prowls around like a roaring lion looking for someone to devour" **(NIV)**.

In some cases, the psychics themselves are deceived, not knowing the true source of the information they receive. Whatever the case and wherever the source of the information, nothing connected to spiritism, witchcraft, or astrology is a godly means of discovering information. How does God want us to discern His will for our life? God's plan is simple, yet powerful and effective: study the Bible: (Got Questions Ministries, 2016).

> **II Timothy 3:16-17** - "All Scripture is God-breathed and is useful for teaching, rebuking, correcting and training in righteousness, so that the servant of God may be thoroughly equipped for every good work" **(NIV)**.

And pray for wisdom:

> **James 1:5** - "If any of you lacks wisdom, you should ask God, who gives generously to all without finding fault, and it will be given to you" **(NIV)**.

You are born with a spirit. And because part of our being is eternal there is ever present a spirit.

Part of this spirit has an intuitiveness nature about it which the scriptures call discernment. Your intuition has always been a part of you. Whether you consciously use it or not, you rely on it to some degree in your everyday life. This is whether you become a Christian or not. Thus, my interest in writing about our Spirit and thusly, Spirit to Spirit.

CHAPTER 1

"In the beginning" - "God"

"In the beginning ..." is when time began! There was no time before time was created! Time is actually a created entity. A study of this verse reveals that God created time, space, and matter on the first day of Creation Week. No one of these can have a meaningful existence without the others.

> **Genesis 1:1** - "In the beginning God created the heavens and the earth" (**NIV**).

God created the space-mass-time universe. Space and matter must exist in time, and time requires space and matter. Time is only meaningful if physical entities exist and events transpire during time.

> In **Psalm 90:2**, we read: "Before the mountains were born or you brought forth the whole world, from everlasting to everlasting you are God" (**NIV**).

So, what was "before" creation? God existing from everlasting to everlasting, God existing in eternity.

Genesis 1:1 is one of the most consequential verses/sentences ever written! In the beginning, the verse tells us, there was nothing else besides the Almighty Himself. We read nothing of angels, human beings, or any physical material. Even time itself did not exist before the Creator acted to bring something out of nothing. **Hebrews 11** tells us:

> **Hebrews 11:3** - "By faith we understand that the universe was formed at God's command, so that what is seen was not made out of what is visible" (**NIV**).

Unlike His creation, however, our Creator depends on nothing outside Himself for His existence. He is self-existent, having the power of being in Himself. Do you remember what God said to Moses when he asked God who he should say sent him to lead his people out of Egypt's oppression?

> **Exodus 3:14** - "God said to Moses, "I AM WHO I AM. This is what you are to say to the Israelites: 'I AM has sent me to you'" **(NIV)**.

God is the great "I AM." He exists in eternity. He was not created.

> **Revelation 1:8** - "I am the Alpha and the Omega," says the Lord God, "who is, and who was, and who is to come, the Almighty" **(NIV)**.

Isaiah 43 records these words from God:

> **Isaiah 43:10** - "You are my witnesses," declares the LORD, "and my servant whom I have chosen, so that you may know and believe me and understand that I am he. Before me no god was formed, nor will there be one after me" **(NIV)**.

In other words, it's a mistake to talk about what God was doing "before creation" because the concept of time, before, during, and after did not come to be until Day One of Creation Week. God exists; **HE IS** and **HE IS** the eternal self-existent One. **HE IS** outside of time (Ham, 2012).

The climax of God's creative work was His extraordinary creation of man.

> **Genesis 2:7** - "The LORD God formed the man from the dust of the ground and breathed into his nostrils the breath of life, and the man became a living being" **(NIV)**.

The supreme Creator of heaven and earth did two things in creating man. First, He formed him from the very dust of the ground, a lifeless human body lying on the ground. Secondly, He breathed His own breath into the nostrils of Adam. This distinguished man from all of God's other creatures. Man is more than "dust" or physical substance. Man has a spirit. God is the Source of life, and He directly placed life within man. This breath of life is seen again in:

> **John 20:22** - "And with that he breathed on them and said, 'Receive the Holy Spirit'" as Jesus imparts new life to His disciples" **(NIV).**

God did not come into existence. He has always been in existence. The Bible says that He has always existed: **Psalm 90:2** - "... even from everlasting to everlasting, you are God", and **Psalm 93:2** - "Your throne is established from of old; you are from everlasting" **(NIV).**

Quite simply, God has no beginning and no end. So, when we ask how did God come into being, the answer is that He did not. He always was (Slick, 2017).

So, what is the breath of God? It is the life and power of God, given to man to animate him. The Hebrew word for spirit means "wind, breath, air, and spirit." The life of God lives on and on; the immaterial part of man was designed to live eternally. The only question is where will we live?

> **Acts 17:22-34** - "So Paul, standing before the council, addressed them as follows: "Men of Athens, I notice that you are very religious in every way, for as I was walking along I saw your many shrines. And one of your altars had this inscription on it: 'To an Unknown God.' This God, whom you worship without knowing, is the one I'm telling you about. "He is the God who made the world and everything in it. Since he is Lord of heaven and earth, he doesn't live in man-made temples, and human hands can't serve his needs—for he has no needs. He himself gives life and breath to everything, and he satisfies every need. From one man he created all the nations throughout the whole earth. He

3

decided beforehand when they should rise and fall, and he determined their boundaries. "His purpose was for the nations to seek after God and perhaps feel their way toward him and find him—though he is not far from any one of us. For in him we live and move and exist. As some of your own poets have said, 'We are his offspring.' And since this is true, we shouldn't think of God as an idol designed by craftsmen from gold or silver or stone." God overlooked people's ignorance about these things in earlier times, but now he commands everyone everywhere to repent of their sins and turn to him. For he has set a day for judging the world with justice by the man he has appointed, and he proved to everyone who this is by raising him from the dead." When they heard Paul speak about the resurrection of the dead, some laughed in contempt, but others said, "We want to hear more about this later." That ended Paul's discussion with them, but some joined him and became believers. Among them were Dionysius, a member of the council, a woman named Damaris, and others with them" (**NLT**).

What is the breath of life?

Humanity has one characteristic that other living creatures lack. Job's young friend Elihu describes this extra element in:

> **Job 32:8**: "But there is a spirit in man, and the breath of the Almighty gives him understanding" (**KJV**).

When God breathed the breath of life into Adam, he must also have imparted a spirit, an essence, that gave humans all the abilities beyond what animals have.

The apostle Paul also mentions this in the New Testament:

> **I Corinthians 2:11** - For what man knoweth the things of a man, save the spirit of man which is in him? even

so the things of God knoweth no man, but the Spirit of God" (**KJV**)?

This "spirit in man" endows humans with the ability to understand, reason, plan, and create. It joins with the physical brain and assists in our thinking. The Bible often uses the word "spirit" to refer to a person's mind, intelligence, or attitude.

What happens to this spirit in man when we die? Wise Solomon had the answer:

> **Ecclesiastes 12:7** - "Then the dust will return to the earth as it was, and the spirit will return to God who gave it" (**KJV**).

Why does God take it back? Because it is a perfect recording of each person's entire life! All the person's memories, actions, words, attitudes, strengths, weaknesses, victories, defeats, decisions, and plans are recorded by man's spirit!

> **Psalm 42:7** - "Deep calls unto deep at the noise of Your waterfalls; All Your waves and billows have gone over me" (**KJV**).

This phrase, "deep calls unto deep" is communication through prayer from deep recesses of the heart/mind of a man (a secluded or secret place) to the heart/mind of God. We may feel a need for this "deep" communication in times of dire need or suffering (waves and billows or tempestuous times):

> **Psalm 92:5** - "O Lord, how great are thy works! and thy thoughts are very deep" (**KJV**).

> **Psalm 130:1** - "Out of the depths have I cried unto thee, O Lord" (**KJV**).

Paul, the Apostle, had a face-to-face encounter with the Lord Jesus Christ and was left blinded by the occasion:

> **Acts 9:3-9** - "And as he journeyed, he came near Damascus: and suddenly there shined round about him a light from heaven:And he fell to the earth, and heard a voice saying unto him, Saul, Saul, why persecutest thou me? And he said, Who art thou, Lord? And the Lord said, I am Jesus whom thou persecutest: it is hard for thee to kick against the pricks. And he trembling and astonished said, Lord, what wilt thou have me to do? And the Lord said unto him, Arise, and go into the city, and it shall be told thee what thou must do. And the men which journeyed with him stood speechless, hearing a voice, but seeing no man. And Saul arose from the earth; and when his eyes were opened, he saw no man: but they led him by the hand, and brought him into Damascus. And he was three days without sight, and neither did eat nor drink" (**KJV**).

After having become more deeply acquainted with Lord Jesus Christ, and having been baptized in the Holy Spirit, Paul began to learn of wonderful things:

> **I Corinthians 2:9-11** - "But, as it is written, "What no eye has seen, nor ear heard, nor the heart of man conceived, what God has prepared for those who love him," God has revealed to us through the Spirit. For the Spirit searches everything, even the depths of God. For what person knows a man's thoughts except the spirit of the man which is in him? So also no one comprehends the thoughts of God except the Spirit of God" (**KJV**).

From what we can find in the Bible, "deep calling unto deep" could very well mean the heart of man calling out to the heart of God. Perhaps including the fact that the heart of God calls out to the hearts of humans in the hope that they will seek Him out and find Him.

> **Genesis 1:31** - "And God saw everything that he had made, and, behold, it was very good. And the evening and the morning were the sixth day" **(KJV)**.

Everything was very good, but why has human history been a recording of violence, disease, anguish of spirit? Why is there so much bitterness, anger, prejudice, resentment, doubt, self-pity, vanity, envy, greed, jealousy, pride, and lust? Nowhere in God's Word are these called good or even acceptable.

While spirit cannot be seen, we can see the effects of spirit. It is not a coincidence that the word for "spirit," can also be translated as "wind" or "breath":

> **Job 32:8** - "But it is the spirit in a person, the breath of the Almighty, that gives them understanding as quoted above, parallels the spirit in man to "the breath of the Almighty" **(NIV)**.

We cannot see the moving air molecules in wind, but we can observe leaves and branches being moved and know that wind is present. In the dry areas of the West, tumbleweeds roll along and dust-devils form, spin, and disintegrate, revealing that the wind is at work.

> **I Corinthians 2:10-12** - "These are the things God has revealed to us by his Spirit. The Spirit searches all things, even the deep things of God. For who knows a person's thoughts except their own spirit within them? In the same way no one knows the thoughts of God except the Spirit of God. What we have received is not the spirit of the world, but the Spirit who is from God, so that we may understand what God has freely given us" **(NIV)**.

We see three things here:

- There is a spirit in man that enables him to understand physical things.
- God reveals to man through His Spirit, which enables man to penetrate the deep, spiritual things of God.
- We have received the Spirit that is from God, and there is a spirit of this world.

Here, Paul shows at least three different spirits: the spirit in man, the Spirit of God, and the spirit of this world (Ritenbaugh, 2007).

When we believed in the Lord Jesus Christ, some marvelous things happened to us. We were justified by God, forgiven of our sins, and saved from perdition. How we praise God for these wonderful gifts! But as wonderful as each gift is, something more happened when we received Christ: a union and mingling of God's divine Spirit with our human spirit. This is a profound fact that we can enjoy today in our daily experience.

> **Romans 8:16** - "The Spirit Himself witnesses with our spirit that we are children of God" **(KJV)**.

This indicates the mingling of the Lord as the Spirit with our spirit. Our spirit has been regenerated by the Spirit of God. For our being born again:

> **John 3:6** - "That which is born of the flesh is flesh; and that which is born of the Spirit is spirit" **(KJV)**.

And is one with our spirit:

> **Romans 8:16** - "The Spirit itself beareth witness with our spirit, that we are the children of God" **(KJV)**.

This realization of the Lord, who became the life-giving Spirit through resurrection:

I Corinthians 15:45 - "And so it is written, the first man Adam was made a living soul; the last Adam was made a quickening spirit" **(KJV)**.

The Lord who is now with our spirit:

II Timothy 4:22 - "The Lord Jesus Christ be with thy spirit. Grace be with you. Amen" **(KJV)**.

This blended spirit is often referred to in Paul's Epistles:

Romans 8:4-6 - "That the righteousness of the law might be fulfilled in us, who walk not after the flesh, but after the Spirit. For they that are after the flesh do mind the things of the flesh; but they that are after the Spirit the things of the Spirit. For to be carnally minded is death; but to be spiritually minded is life and peace" **(KJV)**.

Conclusion:

There never was a time when He was not, and there never will be a time when He will not be.

As dependent creatures, we rely on the Lord for our standards of right and wrong, our knowledge, and much more. We know our place in the universe only when we remember that He is our Creator and we are His creatures. From this biblical perspective do we begin our journey:

HE IS outside of time!

CHAPTER 2

Kindred Spirits

Finding a kindred spirit is one of the most joyous experiences a human can have. How many do you have? For human beings, relationships are the most important aspects of life. We are social animals, so the connections we make with others can give our life more meaning and make our journey happier. Particularly, when we find our kindred souls.

Definition of Kindred - "Of a similar nature or character" (Dictionary, 2019). What are Kindred Spirits or what is a Kindred Soul exactly? Kindred spirits come in all shapes and sizes, representing all types of relationships. It's true that more often than not, they are a close friend, family member or a love interest. But technically, a kindred spirit or soul can be someone you only met once, but they just "got" you in that moment. Of course, when we naturally have a deep connection like this, we like to keep these people in our life, when possible.

Kindred souls are the people in our lives who just "get us". They seem to think about things in the same way as us and usually have the same values. While a kindred soul might be very different from us and have different interests, passions, vocations, and hobbies, there is still an underlying understanding and a shared way of viewing the world.

Many of our dearest friends are kindred souls. But we can meet a new one at any time. When you meet someone new and just 'click' straight away, you are probably meeting with a kindred soul.

Kindred soul relationships often stand the test of time. These are the people who we can rely on in troubled times and who are ready to share our joy when things go well. We may not see them often, but when we do, we pick up just where we left off as if no time had passed at all.

Why Does Mary Visit Her Cousin Elizabeth?

Mary, expecting a son by the Holy Spirit, traveled to a town 80 miles away to visit her cousin Elizabeth. For Mary, the trip would have been especially grueling via a donkey on poor roads and no way to get comfortable. Why does she do it? Well, think about what has just happened: She's been told that she is pregnant by the power of the Holy Spirit. She's also learned that her cousin Elizabeth, believed to be too old to conceive, is expecting as well. Mary must have been bursting to talk to a woman who could personally understand her excitement, her wonder, and probably her nervousness, too (Moyer 2018).

I am sure Mary felt all kinds of emotions when the angel told her she was going to conceive a son by the Holy Spirit. On the journey from Nazareth to the hill country of Judea, did the young Mary agonize over how she would tell Elizabeth about her own pregnancy? Probably! Immediately after Mary greeted her, Elizabeth blessed the young girl as the mother of her Lord. The story Mary undoubtedly rehearsed over and over in her mind to tell Elizabeth was not necessary. Elizabeth already knew.

God showed the tenderness of HIS heart, who knew that a young, frightened girl would need the encouragement and support of an older confidant. God didn't send just any woman to encourage Mary. He sent her a KINDRED SOUL. Someone who had also experienced the miraculous hand of God in an unexpected pregnancy. Someone who understood her circumstances. Someone who shared her same fears. Someone who understood the true favor of the Most High God on their lives.

> **Luke 1:39-45** - "At that time Mary got ready and hurried to a town in the hill country of Judea, where she entered Zechariah's home and greeted Elizabeth. When Elizabeth heard Mary's greeting, the baby leaped in her womb, and Elizabeth was filled with the Holy Spirit. In a loud voice she exclaimed: "Blessed are you among women and blessed is the child you will bear! But why am I so favored, that the

mother of my Lord should come to me? As soon as the sound of your greeting reached my ears, the baby in my womb leaped for joy. Blessed is she who has believed that the Lord would fulfill his promises to her!" (**NIV**).

I Samuel 18:1 - "And it came to pass, when he had made an end of speaking unto Saul, that the soul of Jonathan was knit with the soul of David, and Jonathan loved him as his own soul" (**KJV**).

Kindred spirits affirm our purpose. Kindred spirits challenge us to live beyond our own limitations and trust in the God who is HUGE! Our journeys of faith are so much richer and deeper when we are blessed by kindred souls who walk alongside with us, through laughter and tears, joy and sorrow, wholeness and brokenness. Ultimately, kindred spirits speak blessing and purpose over us. Has God sent a Kindred Spirit into your life? If not, pray for one.

God did not make us to be alone. To that end, He designed relationships, not just of the marital and familial kind, but friendships as well. Friendships fill the gaps in our lives, providing us with a variety of support, love, and camaraderie. Not only that, but God has left us written testaments to the power of friendship, and of what it looks like at its best, so that we can know how to go about being a friend.

When two people are connected, with a bond from the soul so strongly that the souls become one, they each feel the other's pain and happiness. KINDRED SPIRITS are two people that make a special connection by sharing a bond that has joined them by the means of an experience or experiences that have drawn them together on a higher level of consciousness.

If two people are in a dramatic situation where it is necessary to depend on each other in order to survive the situation, or one having to rescue the other, they would become bonded as KINDRED SPIRITS. Sometimes, a couple will meet that had both come from very bad past situations in a relationship; then, a bond is formed because a mutual understanding of what the other had been through, that bond will be as KINDRED SPIRITS. Some kindred spirit relationships are meant to be just for a period of time in our lives, while others are meant to last a lifetime. Members of our family can easily become kindred spirits because of shared lives and experiences.

Understanding the Kindred Spirit

A kindred spirit is someone that, from the very first moment you meet, you have a feeling that they understand everything about you, that they "get you" and you them. Regardless of your hobbies, interests, passions, backgrounds, and more, a kindred spirit is someone who will look at you from across the room and make you feel that you are not alone. Those friends and loved ones closest to you?

More likely than not, those are kindred spirit/souls. However, some kindred spirits/souls enter our lives for just a moment, or a single period. The length of a relationship does not define a kindred spirit/soul.

It's about the innate connection.

Kindred spirits come in all shapes and sizes, representing all types of relationships. It's true that more often than not, they are a close friend, family member or a love interest. Of course, when we naturally have a deep connection like this, we like to keep these people in our life. But that doesn't always happen for many different reasons (Lynch, 2014).

SIGNS OF A KINDRED SPIRIT

1. *You Have Similar Principles*

This isn't about politics, left or right. This is about the way you view life and humanity, and while you and your friends may have your general agreements and disagreements on certain issues, your kindred spirit will generally understand the world the same way that you do. The bigger things in life will never be a point of contention, and you live your lives in a similar way, which is why you connect as intimately as you do.

2. *You Have Mutual Respect*

No good relationship can exist without respect coming from both sides. And this respect transcends politics and petty opinions, no matter what you say, your kindred spirit will understand where you are coming from and give you the respect you deserve. Both of you know that support and encouragement is what the other person needs.

3. *They teach you*

While a kindred spirit will never let you down, they will be honest when necessary. This means they can teach you new ways of living, being, and thinking. They can help you to look at things in a more objective way. A kindred friendship is not always sweetness and light. You are here to help each other develop spiritually and that takes work. However, the relationship will always feel supportive even when you are working together on difficult issues.

4. *They can challenge you spiritually and make you reach higher.*

Learn the difference between someone who challenges you and someone who is unhealthy for you. There can be a lot of missed opportunities for soul growth if we give up too soon! Some people really are here to teach us patience when we want to walk away. We may have a soul agreement with someone to help us on our spiritual journey, testing us in ways we have never been tested. Once we learn how to heal and evolve the situation; it morphs, we change, and we become unstuck. Our view of the next life task becomes much more positive with every soul accomplishment.

5. *You share life themes and challenges.*

You've probably been through some of the same life tests and themes. You have empathy and compassion for each other that reaches a deeper understanding, and you recognize their light because it matches your own.

6. *They help you move forward on your path*

Often kindred spirits experience similar challenges and tests in life. If you are experiencing a challenge, such as illness, bereavement or depression, you will probably have at least one kindred friend or relative who has been through something similar. They have so much understanding and empathy for your situation that they are able to help you through the challenge. Similarly, you will be able to help others when they go through some challenges that you have experienced.

7. *You enhance one another's lives*

Your kindred spirit will be easy to be with because you can be totally yourself with them. No need to put on a mask or hide your truth from your kindred friend, they'll most likely see right through it. Your skills, strengths, and passions probably complement each other, for example, one may be practical and one a dreamer, or one grows flowers and the other is a flower arranger. It's very possible you have similar business or academic dreams and interests. Kindred spirits often form businesses together as they have complementary skills, respect for one another, and a strong enough relationship to cope with the ups and downs of business.

8. *Understanding Beyond the Need for Words*

It's almost like you understand exactly what each other is thinking. Feelings are complex, hard to describe, and much like an exchange of energy that can't be put into words. But somehow, you "get" your partner's feelings, even if you can't articulate them. A simple glance at one another will tell you everything you need to know in any given situation or circumstance. You'll likely know that your partner is uncomfortable before they know they are themselves! It's a special connection.

9. *You match energetically*

That feeling of having known someone for a lifetime, even if you have only just met comes from an energetic match. You and your kindred spirit will vibrate at the same frequency. This means you are always at the same or similar level. Because you are at a similar spiritual level, you have an understanding and can grow together each step of the way. While some other relationships are predestined to challenge us strongly, and may, therefore, be problematic, our kindred friends are more of a support network.

Closing Thoughts

Being with your kindred spirit always feels wonderful. Spending time in their company will usually leave you feeling peaceful and uplifted. Even when one or the other of you are going through difficult times, you will feel comforted by each other's presence. These kinds of friendships and relationships are golden and we should do everything in our power to nurture them carefully throughout our lives (Brown, 2018).

More than anything else, our relationships give us meaning and depth in our lives. We are social creatures who live and die by the connections we build with those around us. They can be our sources of happiness and joy, and in some cases, our reason for living. But there are some people we'll connect with much more intimately and deeply than most. These are our kindred spirits.

It's our relationships that give meaning to our lives.

CHAPTER 3

David and Jonathan

King David is one of the most well-known figures in Jewish history. He was the second King of Israel and was known by many titles: David the conqueror, David the pious man, David the singer, and David the shepherd. Not only was he acclaimed as a warrior, a musician and a poet, he is credited with composing many of the psalms in the Bible, chanted in prayer by Jews everywhere up to this very day. He also was a descendant of Judah as well as Ruth, and was promised by God that his children would rule Israel forever.

Jonathan was a ruddy, young shepherd and a courageous warrior who had returned victorious from battle. He was the eldest son of King Saul, Israel's first king. David was taken to see King Saul after beheading Goliath, and Jonathan took an immediate liking to the young hero. As the Bible says,

"The soul of Jonathan was knit to the soul of David". Scholars estimate that Jonathan was at least 28 years of age when David killed Goliath and David was likely about 18 years of age, 10 years younger.

Love and respect for each other began at this time: "When David finished speaking with Saul, Jonathan's soul became bound up with the soul of David; Jonathan loved David as himself". Their story gets more chapters in the Bible than any other human love story.

How did their covenant of friendship form so quickly? The answer has to do with the basis for that friendship. Consider some background. Jonathan was living through a difficult time. His father, King Saul, had been changing over the years, and ever for the worse. Once a humble, obedient man of faith, Saul had become an arrogant, disobedient king as observed:

I Samuel 15:17-19 - "And Samuel said, When thou wast little in thine own sight, wast thou not made the head of the tribes of Israel, and the LORD anointed thee king over Israel? And the LORD sent thee on a journey, and said, Go and utterly destroy the sinners the Amalekites, and fight against them until they be consumed. Wherefore then didst thou not obey the voice of the LORD, but didst fly upon the spoil, and didst evil in the sight of the LORD" **(KJV)**?

I Samuel 15:26 - "And Samuel said unto Saul, I will not return with thee: for thou hast rejected the word of the LORD, and the LORD hath rejected thee from being king over Israel" **(KJV)**.

That background may help us to understand what drew Jonathan to young David. Jonathan recognized David's great faith. Jonathan and David had much in common: strong faith in Jehovah and deep love for Him. Unlike soldiers in Saul's army, David was undaunted by Goliath's colossal size. He reasoned that going into battle bearing Jehovah's name made him more powerful than Goliath with all his weapons:

I Samuel 17:45-47 - "Then said David to the Philistine, Thou comest to me with a sword, and with a spear, and with a shield: but I come to thee in the name of the LORD of hosts, the God of the armies of Israel, whom thou hast defied. This day will the LORD deliver thee into mine hand; and I will smite thee, and take thine head from thee; and I will give the carcases of the host of the Philistines this day unto the fowls of the air, and to the wild beasts of the earth; that all the earth may know that there is a God in Israel. And all this assembly shall know that the LORD saveth not with sword and spear: for the battle is the LORD's, and he will give you into our hands" **(KJV)**.

Years earlier, Jonathan had reasoned similarly. He was sure that two men, he and his armor-bearer, could attack and defeat an entire garrison of armed soldiers. Why? "Nothing can hinder Jehovah." Jonathan said:

> **I Samuel 14:6** - "And Jonathan said to the young man that bare his armour, Come, and let us go over unto the garrison of these uncircumcised: it may be that the LORD will work for us: for there is no restraint to the LORD to save by many or by few" (**KJV**).

My supposition is their spirits were touched by God and they consequently were joined, SPIRIT TO SPIRIT! That was the ideal basis for friendship between the two men. Even though Jonathan was a mighty prince, while David was a humble shepherd, those differences between them did not matter because they had a "KINDRED" connection:

Spirit to Spirit

A good friendship such as theirs thrives on open communication, not on secrets and lies. How might learning of David's prospects have affected Jonathan? What if Jonathan had cherished a hope of becoming king one day and righting his father's wrongs? The Bible tells us nothing about any internal struggle Jonathan may have had; it tells only of what truly matters, Jonathan's loyalty and his faith. He could see that Jehovah's spirit was with David:

> **I Samuel 16:1** - "The LORD said to Samuel, "How long will you mourn for Saul, since I have rejected him as king over Israel? Fill your horn with oil and be on your way; I am sending you to Jesse of Bethlehem. I have chosen one of his sons to be king" (**NIV**).

> **I Samuel 16:11-13** - "So he asked Jesse, "Are these all the sons you have?" "There is still the youngest," Jesse answered. "He is tending the sheep." Samuel said, "Send for him; we will not sit down until he arrives." So he sent for him and had him brought in. He was glowing with health and had a fine appearance and handsome features.

Then the LORD said, "Rise and anoint him; this is the one." So Samuel took the horn of oil and anointed him in the presence of his brothers, and from that day on the Spirit of the LORD came powerfully upon David. Samuel then went to Ramah" **(NIV)**.

Jonathan fulfilled his oath and continued to view David not as his rival, but as his friend. Jonathan wanted to see Jehovah's will done (Watch Tower, 2018).

In their relationship we can see at least three qualities of Jonathan being a KINDRED SPIRIT to David. First, they sacrificed for one another.

I Samuel 18:4 - "Jonathan stripped himself of the robe that was on him and gave it to David, with his armor, including his sword and his bow and his belt" **(NASB)**.

Jonathan gave David his clothes and military garb. The significance of this gift was that Jonathan recognized that David would one day be king of Israel. Rather than being envious or jealous, Jonathan submitted to God's will and sacrificed his own right to the throne.

Second, in:

I Samuel 19:1-3 - "Now Saul told Jonathan his son and all his servants to put David to death. But Jonathan, Saul's son, greatly delighted in David. Jonathan told David saying, "Saul my father is seeking to put you to death. Now therefore, please be on guard in the morning, and stay in a secret place and hide yourself. I will go out and stand beside my father in the field where you are, and I will speak with my father about you; if I find out anything, then I will tell you" **(NASB)**.

This passage speaks of Jonathan's loyalty toward and defense of David. King Saul told his followers to kill David as he feared David wanted his throne. Despite knowing that David posed a potential threat to his own place in line to the crown, Jonathan rebuked his father and recalled David's faithfulness to him in killing Goliath.

In **I Samuel**, we read of a plan concocted by Jonathan to reveal his father's plans toward David. Jonathan was going to practice his archery. If he told his servant that the arrows he shot were to the side of the target, David was safe. If Jonathan told his servant that the arrows were beyond the target, David was to leave and not return. Jonathan told the servant that the arrows were beyond the target, meaning that David should flee. After releasing his servant, Jonathan found David and the two men cried together.

The friendship between David and Jonathan was also covenantal in nature. In:

> **I Samuel 18:1-5** - "After David had finished talking with Saul, Jonathan became one in spirit with David, and he loved him as himself. From that day Saul kept David with him and did not let him return home to his family. And Jonathan made a covenant with David because he loved him as himself. Jonathan took off the robe he was wearing and gave it to David, along with his tunic, and even his sword, his bow and his belt. Whatever mission Saul sent him on, David was so successful that Saul gave him a high rank in the army. This pleased all the troops, and Saul's officers as well" (**NIV**).

We read of David and Jonathan forming an agreement. In this agreement, Jonathan was to be second in command in David's future reign, and David was to protect Jonathan's family (Got Questions, 2015).

> **I Samuel 20:4** - "Jonathan said to David, "Whatever you want me to do, I'll do for you" (**NIV**).

> **I Samuel 20:16-17** - "So Jonathan made a covenant with the house of David, saying, "May the LORD call David's enemies to account." And Jonathan had David reaffirm his

oath out of love for him, because he loved him as he loved himself" (**NIV**).

I Samuel 23:16-18 - "And Saul's son Jonathan went to David at Horesh and helped him find strength in God. "Don't be afraid," he said. "My father Saul will not lay a hand on you. You will be king over Israel, and I will be second to you. Even my father Saul knows this." The two of them made a covenant before the LORD. Then Jonathan went home, but David remained at Horesh" (**NIV**).

David never forgot his vow to Jonathan. Years later he sought out and took care of Jonathan's disabled son, Mephibosheth: (Got Questions, 2015)

II Samuel 9:1-13 - "David asked, "Is there anyone still left of the house of Saul to whom I can show kindness for Jonathan's sake?" Now there was a servant of Saul's household named Ziba. They summoned him to appear before David, and the king said to him, "Are you Ziba?" "At your service," he replied. The king asked, "Is there no one still alive from the house of Saul to whom I can show God's kindness?" Ziba answered the king, "There is still a son of Jonathan; he is lame in both feet." "Where is he?" the king asked. Ziba answered, "He is at the house of Makir son of Ammiel in Lo Debar." So King David had him brought from Lo Debar, from the house of Makir son of Ammiel. When Mephibosheth son of Jonathan, the son of Saul, came to David, he bowed down to pay him honor. David said, "Mephibosheth!" "At your service," he replied. "Don't be afraid," David said to him, "for I will surely show you kindness for the sake of your father Jonathan. I will restore to you all the land that belonged to your grandfather Saul, and you will always eat at my table." Mephibosheth bowed down and said, "What is your servant, that you should notice a dead dog like me?" Then the king summoned Ziba, Saul's steward, and said to him, "I have given your master's grandson everything that belonged to Saul and his family. You and your sons and your servants are to farm the land for him and bring in the crops, so that your master's grandson may be provided for. And Mephibosheth, grandson of your master, will always eat at my table." (Now Ziba had fifteen sons and twenty servants.) Then Ziba said to the king, "Your servant will do whatever my lord the king commands his servant to do." So Mephibosheth ate at David's table like one of the king's sons. Mephibosheth had a young son named Mika, and all the members of Ziba's household were servants of Mephibosheth. And Mephibosheth lived in Jerusalem, because he always ate at the king's table; he was lame in both feet" (**NIV**).

Clearly, David had learned much from Jonathan's loyalty and honor and his willingness to stay loyal to a friend even when such loyalty came at a high price. Will we learn such lessons as well?

Can we seek out friends like Jonathan? Can we show such friendship ourselves? If we help our friends to build and strengthen their faith in the Lord, if we put our loyalty to Him first, and if we remain loyal instead of seeking our own interests, we will be the kind of friend that Jonathan was. And we will imitate his faith.

Over the years, some have implied that David and Jonathan had a homosexual relationship. This denies the very foundation of their friendship. Nothing in the Bible suggests that either Jonathan or David had homosexual leanings or that there was anything sexual about their friendship. To state otherwise is to read something into the account that simply is not there.

David and Goliath

At this time, King Saul was battling the Philistines, longtime enemies of Israel. In the valley of Elah, the two armies were poised for battle, with nothing but a hill separating them. The Philistines vastly outnumbered

Saul's army. A Philistine giant, Goliath, appeared on the hill, and his words came roaring down like thunder:

> **I Samuel 17:8-9** - "Why are you all coming out to fight?" he called. "I am the Philistine champion, but you are only the servants of Saul. Choose one man to come down here and fight me! If he kills me, then we will be your slaves. But if I kill him, you will be our slaves" (**NLT**)!

The sight of the fierce giant, six cubits and a span (about 10 feet) tall, a towering figure on the hill, clad in armour, iron and brass from head to foot, filled the Jews with great terror. There was not a single man in the Israelite camp who dared accept the challenge. Day after day, for 40 days, this mighty giant appeared on the hill to repeat his challenge, morning and evening.

Then, young David, filled with courage, approached the giant with just a staff, a slingshot and five stones. And with one shot, he slew the giant where he stood. He proceeded to cut off his head and presented it to King Saul. The Philistines witnessing this event fled in fear. And David was a national hero.

SPIRIT to SPIRIT

The Traditional Story of King David

In the Hebrew scriptures, **I Samuel** introduces readers to a young man who will capture not only the heart of the nation of Israel, but also the heart of God. The Old Testament Prophet Samuel is sent to Jesse of Bethlehem (a common farmer and shepherd) to anoint one of his sons as the new king, while Israel's first king, Saul, is still living but failing in his duties to follow Samuel's instructions and rebelling against the authority/commandments of God. After Jesse parades nearly all his sons by Samuel, each one rejected as king, he finally brings his youngest, David:

> **I Samuel 16:12** - "And he sent, and brought him in. Now he was ruddy, and withal of a beautiful countenance, and goodly to look to. And the LORD said, Arise, anoint him: for this is he" (**KJV**).

Although David does not look like a king should look, he has the heart of a lion, a courageous spirit, and even more, a deep, unending love for God. Samuel, who has been so depressed over King Saul, finds hope and blessing in the young shepherd from Bethlehem in Judea. After David was anointed:

> **I Samuel 16:13** states, "Then Samuel took the horn of oil, and anointed him in the midst of his brethren: and the Spirit of the LORD came upon David from that day forward. So Samuel rose up, and went to Ramah" (**KJV**).

David was more than just a musician; he had the heart of a warrior & a set of shepherding skills on the masters' level.

The news for King Saul, however, is not at all positive. While David receives the blessings of the Holy Spirit,

> **I Samuel 16:14** - "Now the Spirit of the LORD had departed from Saul, and an evil spirit from the LORD tormented him" (**NIV**).

Saul began to experience periods of mental and emotional suffering, brought on by either a bipolar disorder or an evil spirit (according to the biblical text). One of his servants remembers that David is an excellent musician and recommends Saul employ him as an armor-bearer (the one who carried a large shield and other weapons for the king) and a musical balm of sorts for his tortuous episodes.

> **I Samuel 16:23** states, "Whenever the spirit from God came on Saul, David would take up his lyre and play. Then relief would come to Saul; he would feel better, and the evil spirit would leave him" (**NIV**).

Psalm 23:6 - "Surely your goodness and love will follow me all the days of my life, and I will dwell in the house of the LORD forever" **(NIV)**.

II Samuel 12:12-13 - "Then David said to Nathan, "I have sinned against the LORD." Nathan replied, "The LORD has taken away your sin. You are not going to die. But because by doing this you have shown utter contempt for the LORD, the son born to you will die" **(NIV)**.

I Samuel 30:6 - "David was greatly distressed because the men were talking of stoning him; each one was bitter in spirit because of his sons and daughters. But David found strength in the LORD his God" **(NIV)**.

I Samuel 18:7-8 - "As they danced, they sang: "Saul has slain his thousands, and David his tens of thousands." Saul was very angry; this refrain displeased him greatly. "They have credited David with tens of thousands," he thought, "but me with only thousands. What more can he get but the kingdom" **(NIV)**?

I Samuel 17:50 - "So David triumphed over the Philistine with a sling and a stone; without a sword in his hand he struck down the Philistine and killed him" **(NIV)**.

I Samuel 16:7 - "The LORD does not look at the things people look at. People look at the outward appearance, but the LORD looks at the heart" **(NIV)**.

David - King of Israel

The book of **II Samuel** begins with David hearing the news that his best friend and God's anointed king have been slaughtered by the Philistines. Stunned, David is also met with news from an Amalekite (a descendant of

Esau, son of Isaac the Patriarch) that the man killed Saul, taking his crown and armband for David. Expecting a reward, instead the soldier receives an execution:

> **II Samuel 1:14** - "David asked him, "Why weren't you afraid to lift your hand to destroy the LORD's anointed" **(NIV)**?

If David was unwilling to hurt God's anointed, why would anyone think that he would be alright with King Saul's assassination?

David thereafter offers a memorial to Saul and Jonathan. For Saul, he sings of him being a mighty warrior; for Jonathan, he sings of him being a faithful brother. One might expect David to be jubilant about Saul's death, but David truly never wanted Saul dead. Scholars have long noted that David's hopes for his enemies was for them either to be removed or to repent. In Saul's case, he definitely wished for the latter. The kingship of David described in **II Samuel 2** is just as exciting and dramatic as his period running away from King Saul. With Samuel's original blessing, David becomes the first king of Judah, but immediately launches into a seven-year civil war with King Saul's son, Ish-Bosheth, that does not end until Saul's son is assassinated in his bed by two Benjamites, the last tribe of Judah and descendants of Jacob the Patriarch.

Expecting a great reward like the previously-mentioned Amalakite, they bring Ish-Bosheth's head to David who immediately executes them for their despicable and criminal activity, saying,

> **II Samuel 4:11** - "How much more when wicked men have killed an innocent man in his own house and on his own bed should I not now demand his blood from your hand and rid the earth of you" **(NIV)**!

David has the men killed, cuts off their feet and hands, and hangs their bodies in shameful display. Later, he buries Ish-Bosheth's head, properly and respectfully in Abner's tomb (Abner was Saul's cousin and commander-in-chief of his army).

With Ish-Bosheth dead, David is offered the crown by the elders of Israel, and recorded by Samuel in:

> **II Samuel 5:4** records, "David was thirty years old when he became king, and he reigned forty years" (**NIV**).

He then conquers Jerusalem, Zion, to which he soon also brings the ark of the covenant. David has hopes to build God's temple in Jerusalem, but that David's offspring will be the one to:

> **II Samuel 7:13** - "He is the one who will build a house for my Name, and I will establish the throne of his kingdom forever" (**NIV**).

The next few chapters detail and discuss the tremendous victories for David against the Philistines, the Geshurites, the Gezites, the Jebusites, and the Amalekites.

> In **II Samuel 6:16** - "As the ark of the LORD was entering the City of David, Michal daughter of Saul watched from a window. And when she saw King David leaping and dancing before the LORD, she despised him in her heart" (**NIV**).

King David, one of the most virtuous men in the Bible, forgets his place, his responsibilities to God and to his subjects, and starts a love affair with Bathsheba, the wife of Uriah the Hittite, one of his Mighty Warriors.

David & Bathsheba

While relaxing at the palace, King David happens to see beautiful Bathsheba, the daughter of Eliam and future mother of King palace Solomon, bathing upon her roof and the temptation is too tempting for him.

II Samuel 11:4 records: "Then David sent messengers to
get her. She came to him, and he slept with her. (Now she
was purifying herself from her monthly uncleanness.) Then
she went back home" (**NIV**).

Unfortunately for the pair, Bathsheba becomes pregnant with David's child.

The situation is delicate, at best. Although feminists claim that David
forced Bathsheba, and traditionalists claim that Bathsheba seduced David,
the truth is more one of mutual culpability except, perhaps, that as king and
the model for the Law of God, David had a higher obligation to protect and
not exploit Bathsheba. The text does not lay the blame on any one person
(somewhat like the Fall in Genesis); however, as bad as things are for the
adulterous couple, it is only going to get worse.

David conspires to hide his sin and so, calls Uriah home from the
battlefield and tries to get him to sleep with his wife. Uriah, however, is
too devoted and too lawful to squander his time while his men are dying in
battle. His plans foiled to confuse the paternity of the child, David orders
General Joab, his nephew through David's sister Zeruiah, to place Uriah
in the thick of the most dangerous fighting and then withdraw everyone
but him.

Several things happen because of this. First, poor Uriah gets killed.
Second, Bathsheba mourns for Uriah; there is nothing said about this
being a unified plan. Most likely, it was David's own attempt to protect his
reputation. He quickly moves Bathsheba into the palace and marries her
before the child is born. Third, any loyalty of Joab to David is gone. Rather
than the noble and virtuous warrior of the Lord, now David has become as
bad if not worse than murderous Saul. David's plans soon begin to backfire
upon him.

The Final Years

David's initial zeal for God and for ethical integrity paved the way for his early fame and fortune. David was a man of warfare and blood (according to the scriptures), and God decided that he was not suitable to be the one to build God's temple (that would be placed in the hands of his son, Solomon). David's illicit affair and subsequent devious actions (leading to the assassination of Uriah the Hittite and its cover up) complicated the rest of his reign, along with the rape of Tamar, the murder of Amnon, and the attempted coup of Absalom, among other controversy.

By the end of David's life, he had lost touch with Israelite society and eventually lost political control of it, as well. This led to an attempted coup by his son, Adonijah (whose mother was Haggith, David's fifth wife), who proclaimed himself to be king with the assistance of General Joab and Abiathar the Priest; however, the majority of Israel's institutional agents did not support Adonijah's claim.

The Hebrew scriptures state that the Prophet Nathan went first to Bathsheba to alert her to Adonijah's usurpation of the throne, who then went to her husband, King David, to break the troubling news to him. Eventually, the Prophet Nathan joined the two, and King David officially made Solomon his heir apparent.

> **I Kings 1:30** - "I will surely carry out this very day what I swore to you by the LORD, the God of Israel: Solomon your son shall be king after me, and he will sit on my throne in my place" (**NIV**).

King David died from natural causes and was buried in Jerusalem, and, as suggested in the Hebrew and Greek scriptures, facilitated the establishment of the kingdom of Israel through his piety and lineage.

Before his death, David gave his final admonition to his son, Solomon, saying,

> **I Kings 2:3** - "Keep the charge of the Lord your God: to walk in his ways, to keep his statutes, his commandments, his judgments, and his testimonies, as it is written in the Law of Moses, that you may prosper in all that you do and wherever you turn... for you are a wise man" (**KJV**).

Keep the charge of the Lord your God: to walk in HIS ways!

CHAPTER 4

Naomi and Ruth

One of the ways that God disciplined Israel for her sin was by bringing famine into the land, usually through drought but also by pests such as locusts. During one of these episodes of famine, Elimelech, a man from Bethlehem, took his wife Naomi and his two sons to the neighboring country of Moab. During the ten years the family lived in the land of Moab, Elimelech died leaving Naomi a widow. However, her two sons grew up and married Moabite women. Then, the sons died. Naomi was left with only her daughters-in-law.

The Book of Ruth

Ruth is a book for all times, whether written in post-exilic days or based upon very old oral traditions. It is set in the time of the judges, not the best ones, if we assign it to the period of Gideon and Samson and it attempts to define the rights of widows and aliens within a society fallen upon hard times.

The Book of Leviticus comes to life here, with its injunctions to leave part of the harvest for the needy, and with all of its concern and compassion for the underprivileged within the society. It takes the legalities of the time for granted, as incidental to the unfolding of a Divine pattern within human lives, in the creation of a family tree for King David, with possible intimations of a messianic kingdom. It began with the suffering of Naomi, and ends with her joy. The declaration of Ruth is fulfilled: The destinies of Naomi and Ruth are interlocked, they are now one family and one faith.

Boaz has fulfilled both of their hopes; he has been the redeemer to Naomi, the true husband to Ruth. And the community rejoices.

Certainly, it gives full rights to a Moabite woman who then becomes the ancestress of the royal house of the Jewish people, of King David who comes to represent the messianic ideal, the unity and peace which will embrace all humanity

Naomi and Ruth

The story of Naomi appears in the Bible in the Book of Ruth. Naomi lived during the time of the judges. She was the wife of a man named Elimelech, and they lived in Bethlehem with their two sons, Mahlon and Kilion. Naomi's life illustrates the power of God to bring something good out of bitter circumstances (Got Questions Ministries, 2015).

When a famine hits Judea, Elimelech and Naomi and their two boys relocate to Moab:

> **Ruth 1:1** - "Now it came to pass in the days when the judges ruled, that there was a famine in the land. And a certain man of Bethlehemjudah went to sojourn in the country of Moab, he, and his wife, and his two sons" **(KJV)**.

There, Mahlon and Kilion marry two Moabite women, Orpah and Ruth. After about ten years, tragedy strikes. Elimelech dies, and both of Naomi's sons also die, leaving Naomi, Ruth, and Orpah widows:

> **Ruth 1:3-5** - "And Elimelech Naomi's husband died; and she was left, and her two sons. And they took them wives of the women of Moab; the name of the one was Orpah, and the name of the other Ruth: and they dwelled there about ten years. And Mahlon and Chilion died also both of them; and the woman was left of her two sons and her husband" **(KJV)**.

Naomi, hearing that the famine in Judea was over, decides to return home:

> **Ruth 1:6** - "Then she arose with her daughters in law, that she might return from the country of Moab: for she had heard in the country of Moab how that the LORD had visited his people in giving them bread" **(KJV)**.

Orpah stays in Moab, but Ruth chooses to move to the land of Israel with Naomi. The book of Ruth is the story of Naomi and Ruth returning to Bethlehem and how Ruth married a man named Boaz and bore a son, Obed, who became the grandfather of David and the ancestor of Jesus Christ.

The name *Naomi* means "sweet, pleasant," which gives us an idea of Naomi's basic character. We see her giving her blessing to Ruth and Orpah when she tells them to return to their mothers' homes so that they might find new husbands: she kisses them and asks that the Lord deal kindly with them.

> **Ruth 1:8-14** - "And Naomi said unto her two daughters in law, Go, return each to her mother's house: the LORD deal kindly with you, as ye have dealt with the dead, and with me. The LORD grant you that ye may find rest, each of you in the house of her husband. Then she kissed them; and they lifted up their voice, and wept. And they said unto her, Surely we will return with thee unto thy people. And Naomi said, Turn again, my daughters: why will ye go with me? are there yet any more sons in my womb, that they may be your husbands? Turn again, my daughters, go your way; for I am too old to have an husband. If I should say, I have hope, if I should have an husband also to night, and should also bear sons; Would ye tarry for them till they were grown? would ye stay for them from having husbands? nay, my daughters; for it grieveth me much for your sakes that the hand of the LORD is gone out against me. And they lifted up their voice, and wept

again: and Orpah kissed her mother in law; but Ruth clave unto her" (**KJV**).

But her heartache in Moab was more than Naomi could bear. When she and Ruth arrive in Bethlehem, the women of the town greet Naomi by name, but she cries, "Don't call me Naomi. . . . Call me Mara, because the Almighty has made my life very bitter. I went away full, but the Lord has brought me back empty. Why call me Naomi? The Lord has afflicted me; the Almighty has brought misfortune upon me."

> **Ruth 1:20-21** - "And she said unto them, Call me not Naomi, call me Mara: for the Almighty hath dealt very bitterly with me. I went out full and the LORD hath brought me home again empty: why then call ye me Naomi, seeing the LORD hath testified against me, and the Almighty hath afflicted me" (**KJV**)?

The name Mara means "bitter." The cup of affliction is a bitter cup, but Naomi understood that the affliction came from the God who is sovereign in all things. Little did she know that from this bitter sorrow great blessings would come to her, her descendants, and the world through Jesus Christ. Ruth declares to Naomi:

> **Ruth 1:16** - "But Ruth replied, "Don't urge me to leave you or to turn back from you. Where you go I will go, and where you stay I will stay. Your people will be my people and your God my God" (**NIV**).

Ruth's statement not only proclaims her loyalty to Naomi but her desire to join Naomi's people, the Jewish people. "In the thousands of years since Ruth spoke these words," writes Rabbi Joseph Telushkin, "no one has better defined the combination of peoplehood and religion that characterizes Judaism: 'Your people shall be my people' ('I wish to join the Jewish nation'), 'Your God shall be my God' ('I wish to accept the Jewish religion')" (Pelaia, 2018).

The story of Naomi and her daughter-in-law, Ruth, is one of friendship found in an unlikely place. How many of us have heard the all-too-common jokes made about in-laws, particularly mother-in-laws? And how many of us have ever found a best friend in our mother-in-law? Ruth, married to one of Naomi's sons, did. Years after that son died, along with Naomi's husband and other son, Naomi encouraged her daughters-in-law to go back to their families in Moab. Orpah, one of Naomi's daughters-in-law, left, but not Ruth. Ruth stayed, pledging her life to the now destitute Naomi in:

> **Ruth 1:16-17** - "But Ruth said, "Do not urge me to leave you or turn back from following you; for where you go, I will go, and where you lodge, I will lodge. Your people shall be my people, and your God, my God. Where you die, I will die, and there I will be buried. Thus may the LORD do to me, and worse, if anything but death parts you and me"
> **(NASB)**.

Ruth said, "Don't urge me to leave you or turn back from you. Where you go I will go, and where you stay I will stay." Ruth refused to let Naomi be completely alone, and went with her when she traveled to Bethlehem. She helped her survive as a lone woman in a patriarchal society, gathered food, and eventually had a son that gave Naomi a sense of family again, a son who would go on to be the grandfather of the same David we learned about earlier. Again, this friendship shows us the value of loyalty, of unconditional love and self-sacrifice. Ruth didn't hesitate to give when Naomi was in need. This is the kind of action that creates the strongest of friendships, and gives us a sense of security and we know that when we're in trouble, someone will be there for us.

Where you go I will go

and

Where you stay I will stay.

CHAPTER 5

Elijah and Elisha

Elijah! His name means "The LORD is my God." The message of his life matched his name. It still does today. Not only do we see evidence of this man threaded throughout portions of the Old Testament, but we also find mention of him sprinkled in the New Testament as well. Elijah's name means "Yahweh is my God" and is spelled Elias in some versions of the Bible. The story of his prophetic career in the northern kingdom of Israel during the reigns of Kings Ahab and Ahaziahis is told in **I Kings 17-19** and **II Kings 1-2** in the Old Testament.

Elijah the Tishbite, from the region of Gilead, was one of the two men in the Hebrew Scriptures who did not die but was taken by God; the other was Enoch. Elijah prophesied during the reign of King Ahab of Israel. He performed his first miracles in the town of Zarephath, near Sidon, in the house of a poor widow, where he converted a handful of meal and a little oil into an endless supply and brought back to life the dead child of the widow (Britannica, 2015).

As a prophet, Eliljah adamantly shared God's message and warnings. Often, both came under fire. Sometimes, however, people turned from following false gods and found themselves deep in worship of the Holy One.

> **I Kings 18:21** - "Elijah came near to all the people and said, "How long *will* you hesitate between two opinions? If the LORD is God, follow Him; but if Baal, follow him." But the people did not answer him a word" (**NASB**).

The people didn't say a word.

Jezebel, the wife of King Ahab, was a Phoenician princess, daughter of Ethbaal, king of Sidon. She exerted a strong influence over the king, who granted her unlimited administrative authority. She introduced in Israel the Phoenician pagan cult of the god Baal, a development that was bitterly opposed by the prophet Elijah. Not only did Ahab tolerate the foreign cult introduced by his wife but he also cooperated with her by building a temple for Baal in Samaria and erecting a sacred post.

Time after time in Scripture we see that people leaned their ear toward the Almighty. Include Elijah on this list. Call him a man who heard God.

> **I Kings 19:9** - "Then he came there to a cave and lodged there; and behold, the word of the LORD *came* to him, and He said to him, 'What are you doing here, Elijah?'" (**NASB**).

The narrative in **I Kings** relates how he suddenly appears during Ahab's reign to proclaim a drought in punishment of the cult of Baal that Jezebel was promoting in Israel at Yahweh's expense. Later Elijah meets 450 prophets of Baal in a contest of strength on Mount Carmel to determine which deity is the true God of Israel. Sacrifices are placed on an altar to Baal and one to Yahweh. The pagan prophets' ecstatic appeals to Baal to kindle the wood on his altar are unsuccessful, but Elijah's prayers to Yahweh are answered by a fire on his altar. This outcome is taken as decisive by the Israelites, who slay the priests and prophets of Baal under Elijah's direction. The drought thereupon ends with the falling of rain (Britannica, 2015).

Elijah's deepest prophetic experience takes place on his pilgrimage to Horeb, where he learns that God is not in the storm, the earthquake, or the lightning. Nature, so far from being God's embodiment, is not an adequate symbol. God is invisible and spiritual and is best known in the intellectual word of revelation, as "the still, small voice."

Elijah, the well-known prophet of Israel, was the man who called down the fires of heaven, defeating the prophets of Baal, and the man who caused a drought in Israel for three years through prayer. To help him carry out his work, God saw fit to send Elijah a friend and eventual successor, the younger Elisha. Elijah obeyed God's word and found Elisha, who was plowing with a pair of oxen at the time. Elijah put his cloak around Elisha, a sign that Elijah's responsibilities would fall on Elisha, and Elisha left his oxen and ran after the prophet. Elisha asked only to say goodbye to his family and then would return to Elijah. Elisha went back, slaughtered his oxen and burnt his equipment, gave the meat to the people, then followed Elijah as his servant. Elisha responded to the call immediately. He completely removed himself from his former life, essentially hosting a celebration and leaving himself no option to return to his oxen. Not only did Elisha leave his former life, he became a servant in his new life.

> **I Kings 19:21** - "So Elisha left him and went back. He took his yoke of oxen and slaughtered them. He burned the plowing equipment to cook the meat and gave it to the people, and they ate. Then he set out to follow Elijah and became his servant" **(NIV)**.

It is important to choose friends who are wise and holy and passionate about what they do; after all, we tend to become like our peers. In bringing himself close to Elijah, Elisha prepared himself for his destiny, finding the mentor and friend who would help him become a worthy prophet and servant of God.

Elijah told Elisha that, if he saw Elijah when he was taken, then a double portion of his spirit would belong to Elisha. Elisha did, indeed, see the chariot of fire and horses of fire that separated the men, and he saw Elijah taken to heaven in a whirlwind. Elisha picked up Elijah's cloak and walked to the Jordan River. Elisha struck the water with the cloak, and it divided, just as it had done for Elijah. The other prophets who witnessed this recognized that Elijah's spirit now rested on Elisha. As God had decreed, Elisha would now be His prophet to the people:

> **II Kings 2:1-18** - "And it came about when the LORD was about to take up Elijah by a whirlwind to heaven, that Elijah went with Elisha from Gilgal. Elijah said to Elisha, "Stay

here please, for the LORD has sent me as far as Bethel." But Elisha said, "As the LORD lives and as you yourself live, I will not leave you." So they went down to Bethel. Then the sons of the prophets who *were* at Bethel came out to Elisha and said to him, "Do you know that the LORD will take away your master from over you today?" And he said, "Yes, I know; be still." Elijah said to him, "Elisha, please stay here, for the LORD has sent me to Jericho." But he said, "As the LORD lives, and as you yourself live, I will not leave you." So they came to Jericho. The sons of the prophets who *were* at Jericho approached Elisha and said to him, "Do you know that the LORD will take away your master from over you today?" And he answered, "Yes, I know; be still." Then Elijah said to him, "Please stay here, for the LORD has sent me to the Jordan." And he said, "As the LORD lives, and as you yourself live, I will not leave you." So the two of them went on. Now fifty men of the sons of the prophets went and stood opposite *them* at a distance, while the two of them stood by the Jordan. Elijah took his mantle and folded it together and struck the waters, and they were divided here and there, so that the two of them crossed over on dry ground. When they had crossed over, Elijah said to Elisha, "Ask what I shall do for you before I am taken from you." And Elisha said, "Please, let a double portion of your spirit be upon me." He said, "You have asked a hard thing. *Nevertheless*, if you see me when I am taken from you, it shall be so for you; but if not, it shall not be *so*." As they were going along and talking, behold, *there appeared* a chariot of fire and horses of fire which separated the two of them. And Elijah went up by a whirlwind to heaven. Elisha saw *it* and cried out, "My father, my father, the chariots of Israel and its horsemen!" And he saw Elijah no more. Then he took hold of his own clothes and tore them in two pieces. He also took up the mantle of Elijah that fell from him and returned and stood by the bank of the Jordan. He took the mantle of Elijah that fell from him and struck the waters and said,

"Where is the LORD, the God of Elijah?" And when he also had struck the waters, they were divided here and there; and Elisha crossed over. Now when the sons of the prophets who *were* at Jericho opposite *him* saw him, they said, "The spirit of Elijah rests on Elisha." And they came to meet him and bowed themselves to the ground before him. They said to him, "Behold now, there are with your servants fifty strong men, please let them go and search for your master; perhaps the Spirit of the LORD has taken him up and cast him on some mountain or into some valley." And he said, "You shall not send." But when they urged him until he was ashamed, he said, "Send." They sent therefore fifty men; and they searched three days but did not find him. They returned to him while he was staying at Jericho; and he said to them, "Did I not say to you, 'Do not go'" (**NASB**)?

There, Elijah confessed that he believed himself to be the only faithful prophet remaining. God told Elijah to go back home, anoint Hazael king of Aram, Jehu king of Israel, and Elisha to succeed him as prophet. God said:

> **I Kings 19:17** - "Jehu will put to death any who escape the sword of Hazael, and Elisha will put to death any who escape the sword of Jehu" (**KJV**).

He also reassured Elijah that there were 7,000 remaining who had not bowed to Baal.

Elisha

Elisha, whose name means "God is salvation," was the successor of Elijah in the office of the prophet in Israel:

> **I Kings 19:19-21** - "So he departed thence, and found Elisha the son of Shaphat, who was plowing with twelve yoke of oxen before him, and he with the twelfth: and Elijah

passed by him, and cast his mantle upon him. And he left the oxen, and ran after Elijah, and said, Let me, I pray thee, kiss my father and my mother, and then I will follow thee. And he said unto him, Go back again: for what have I done to thee? And he returned back from him, and took a yoke of oxen, and slew them, and boiled their flesh with the instruments of the oxen, and gave unto the people, and they did eat. Then he arose, and went after Elijah, and ministered unto him" (**KJV**).

II Kings 5:8 - "And it was so, when Elisha the man of God had heard that the king of Israel had rent his clothes, that he sent to the king, saying, Wherefore hast thou rent thy clothes? let him come now to me, and he shall know that there is a prophet in Israel" (**KJV**).

He was called to follow Elijah in:

I Kings 19:19 - "So he departed thence, and found Elisha the son of Shaphat, who was plowing with twelve yoke of oxen before him, and he with the twelfth: and Elijah passed by him, and cast his mantle upon him" (**KJV**).

He spent the next several years as the prophet's protégé, until Elijah was taken into heaven. At that time, Elisha began his ministry, which lasted about 60 years, spanning the reigns of kings Jehoram, Jehu, Jehoahaz and Joash (Got Questions, 2018).

"Who was Elisha in the Bible?"

The initial call of Elisha is instructive. After a mighty display of God's power against the prophets of Baal and a return of the rain after a long drought, Queen Jezebel sought Elijah's life. Afraid, the prophet fled. He was refreshed by an angel and prepared for a forty-day journey to Mount

Horeb. There are many well-known accounts of Elisha's service as prophet. He healed the waters of Jericho;

> **II Kings 2:19-21** - "Now the people of the city said to Elisha, "The location of this city is good, as my lord sees; but the water is bad, and the land is unfruitful." He said, "Bring me a new bowl, and put salt in it." So they brought it to him. Then he went to the spring of water and threw the salt into it, and said, "Thus says the LORD, I have made this water wholesome; from now on neither death nor miscarriage shall come from it" (**NASV**).

And was jeered by youths upon whom he called a curse resulting in their death by mauling bears:

> **II Kings 2:23-25** - "He went up from there to Bethel; and while he was going up on the way, some small boys came out of the city and jeered at him, saying, "Go away, baldhead! Go away, baldhead!" When he turned around and saw them, he cursed them in the name of the LORD. Then two she-bears came out of the woods and mauled forty-two of the boys. From there he went on to Mount Carmel, and then returned to Samaria" (**RSV**).

He multiplied a widow's oil:

> **II Kings 4:1-7** - "Now the wife of a member of the company of prophets cried to Elisha, "Your servant my husband is dead; and you know that your servant feared the LORD, but a creditor has come to take my two children as slaves." Elisha said to her, "What shall I do for you? Tell me, what do you have in the house?" She answered, "Your servant has nothing in the house, except a jar of oil." He said, "Go outside, borrow vessels from all your neighbors, empty vessels and not just a few. Then go in, and shut the door behind you and your children, and start pouring into all

these vessels; when each is full, set it aside." So she left him and shut the door behind her and her children; they kept bringing vessels to her, and she kept pouring. When the vessels were full, she said to her son, "Bring me another vessel." But he said to her, "There are no more." Then the oil stopped flowing. She came and told the man of God, and he said, "Go sell the oil and pay your debts, and you and your children can live on the rest" **(RSV)**.

He prophesied a son for a wealthy Shunammite family who hosted him and later resurrected that same son in **II Kings 4**. Elisha also removed poison from a pot of stew:

> **II Kings 4:38-41** - "When Elisha returned to Gilgal, there was a famine in the land. As the company of prophets was sitting before him, he said to his servant, "Put the large pot on, and make some stew for the company of prophets." One of them went out into the field to gather herbs; he found a wild vine and gathered from it a lapful of wild gourds, and came and cut them up into the pot of stew, not knowing what they were. They served some for the men to eat. But while they were eating the stew, they cried out, "O man of God, there is death in the pot!" They could not eat it. He said, "Then bring some flour." He threw it into the pot, and said, "Serve the people and let them eat." And there was nothing harmful in the pot" **(NIV)**.

And multiplied twenty barley loaves to feed one hundred men:

> **II Kings 4:42-44** - "A man came from Baal-shalishah, bringing food from the first fruits to the man of God: twenty loaves of barley and fresh ears of grain in his sack. Elisha said, "Give it to the people and let them eat." But his servant said, "How can I set this before a hundred people?" So he repeated, "Give it to the people and let them eat, for thus says the LORD, 'They shall eat and have some left.'" He

set it before them, they ate, and had some left, according to the word of the LORD'" **(RSV)**.

He cured Naaman of leprosy in **II Kings 5** and made an ax head float in **II Kings 6**:

> **II Kings 6:1-7** - "Now the company of prophets said to Elisha, "As you see, the place where we live under your charge is too small for us. Let us go to the Jordan, and let us collect logs there, one for each of us, and build a place there for us to live." He answered, "Do so." Then one of them said, "Please come with your servants." And he answered, "I will." So he went with them. When they came to the Jordan, they cut down trees. But as one was felling a log, his ax head fell into the water; he cried out, "Alas, master! It was borrowed." Then the man of God said, "Where did it fall?" When he showed him the place, he cut off a stick, and threw it in there, and made the iron float. He said, "Pick it up." So he reached out his hand and took it" **(RSV)**.

The miracles Elisha performed are, for the most part, acts of helpfulness and blessing. Others strongly resemble some of the miracles of Christ, such as the multiplying of food:

> **Matthew 16:9-10** - "Do you still not perceive? Do you not remember the five loaves for the five thousand, and how many baskets you gathered? Or the seven loaves for the four thousand, and how many baskets you gathered" **(RSV)**?

And the healing of lepers:

> **Luke 17:11-19** - "On the way to Jerusalem Jesus was going through the region between Samaria and Galilee. As he entered a village, ten lepers approached him. Keeping their distance, they called out, saying, "Jesus, Master, have mercy on us!" When he saw them, he said to them, "Go and show

yourselves to the priests." And as they went, they were made clean. Then one of them, when he saw that he was healed, turned back, praising God with a loud voice. He prostrated himself at Jesus' feet and thanked him. And he was a Samaritan. Then Jesus asked, "Were not ten made clean? But the other nine, where are they? Was none of them found to return and give praise to God except this foreigner?" Then he said to him, "Get up and go on your way; your faith has made you well" **(RSV)**.

Elisha seemed to love Elijah like he would a father. He refused to leave Elijah before Elijah was taken into heaven, despite Elijah's telling Elisha to remain behind. Elijah permitted Elisha to stay with him, and he asked what he could do for his protégé before he left. Elisha requested a double portion of Elijah's spirit. This was not a greedy request but rather one indicating that Elisha wanted to be considered as Elijah's son.

As God had decreed, Elisha would now be His prophet to the people. A study of the life of Elisha will reveal the prophet's humility.

> **II Kings 2:9** - "When they had crossed, Elijah said to Elisha, "Tell me, what can I do for you before I am taken from you?" "Let me inherit a double portion of your spirit," Elisha replied" **(NIV)**.

> **II Kings 3:11** - "But Jehoshaphat asked, "Is there no prophet of the LORD here, through whom we may inquire of the LORD?" An officer of the king of Israel answered, "Elisha son of Shaphat is here. He used to pour water on the hands of Elijah" **(KJV)**.

He obviously had a love for the people of Israel:

> **II Kings 8:11-12** - "He stared at him with a fixed gaze until Hazael was embarrassed. Then the man of God began to weep. "Why is my lord weeping?" asked Hazael. "Because I

know the harm you will do to the Israelites," he answered. "You will set fire to their fortified places, kill their young men with the sword, dash their little children to the ground, and rip open their pregnant women" (**NIV**).

Elisha was obedient to God's call, following Elijah eagerly and faithfully. Elisha clearly believed God and trusted Him. Elisha sought after God, and through him God worked powerfully. Their friendship displays another important aspect, the purposeful choosing of friends. Elisha attaches himself to Elijah, imploring the older man not to leave him in:

> **II Kings 2:2** - "And Elijah said unto Elisha, Tarry here, I pray thee; for the LORD hath sent me to Bethel. And Elisha said unto him, As the LORD liveth, and as thy soul liveth, I will not leave thee. So they went down to Bethel" (**KJV**).

Responding to Elijah's declaration that he was leaving for Bethel, Elisha exclaims, "As the Lord lives, and as you yourself live, I will not leave you." Elisha was absolutely devoted to his friend, to his mentor, because he knew the older man would make an excellent guide. It is important to choose friends who are wise and holy and passionate about what they do; after all, we tend to become like our peers. In bringing himself close to Elijah, Elisha prepared himself for his destiny, finding the mentor and friend who would help him become a worthy prophet and servant of God.

Elisha prepared himself for his destiny

CHAPTER 6

Moses and Aaron

Perhaps no person in history, outside of Jesus Christ, has made such a profound impression on the world as Moses, the great lawgiver of Israel. Even so, God is the central focus. From the moment God first appeared to him at the burning bush, Moses consistently turned his eyes toward God. As Moses responded to God in faith, the Lord developed his character as a mighty leader of His people.

It is Moses who leads the Jews out of slavery, unleashes the Ten Plagues against Egypt, guides the freed slaves for forty years in the wilderness, carries down the law from Mount Sinai, and prepares the Jews to enter the land of Canaan. Without Moses, there would be little apart from laws to write about in the last four books of the Torah.

One of the measures taken by the Egyptians to restrict the growth of the Hebrews was to order the death of all newborn Hebrew males. According to tradition, Moses' parents, Amram and Jochebed (whose other children were Aaron and Miriam), hid him for three months and then set him afloat on the Nile in a reed basket daubed with pitch. The child, found by the pharaoh's daughter while bathing, was reared in the Egyptian court. As an adult, Moses delivered an oppressed people from bondage, molded them into a renewed nation and received revelation from God with new moral standards and laws.

God said to Moses, I AM WHO I AM. This is
what you are to say to the Israelites:
I AM has sent me to you

Moses grows up in the Egyptian palace and most likely, Moses was about 25 when he took the inspection tour among his people. And one day he sees an Egyptian beating a Hebrew slave and kills him, burying his body in the sand. As a prince in the court, Moses was probably in excellent physical condition, and apparently he knew the latest methods of combat. The next day, when he is again out among the people, he sees two Hebrews fighting and pulls them apart asking what the problem is. One of them answers by asking if he plans to kill them as he did the Egyptian. Moses then realizes his crime has become known and flees Egypt for Midian (mainly in northwest Arabia) (Bible Study Fellowship, 2009).

In the land of Midian he rescues the daughters of a high priest (named Reuel in Exodus 2 and Jethro afterwards) who gives him his daughter Zipporah as a wife. Moses lives in Midian as a shepherd until he one day encounters a bush which burns with fire but is not consumed. The fire is the angel of God who brings Moses a message that he should return to Egypt to free his people. Moses is not interested and bluntly tells God, "Please send someone else"'

> **Exodus 4:13** - "And he said, O my Lord, send, I pray thee, by the hand of him whom thou wilt send" **(KJV)**.

God is in no mood to be questioned on his choice and makes it clear that Moses will be returning to Egypt. He assures him all will be well and that he will have his brother, Aaron, to help him speak. He will have supernatural powers which will enable him to convince pharaoh that he speaks for God. He also tells Moses, in a passage which has long troubled interpreters of the book, that he will "harden pharaoh's heart" against receiving the message and letting the people go at the same time that he wants pharaoh to accept the message and release his people.

Months later, in the Sinai Desert, Moses climbs Mount Sinai and comes down with the Ten Commandments, only to discover the **Israelite** engaged in an orgy and worshiping a golden calf. The episode is typical: Only at the very moment God or Moses is doing something for them are they loyal believers. The instant God's or Moses' presence is not manifest, the children of Israel revert to immoral, and sometimes idolatrous behavior. Like a true parent, Moses rages at the Jews when they sin, but he never turns against them even when God does. To God's wrathful declaration on one occasion that He will blot out the Jews and make of Moses a new nation, he answers:

> **Exodus 32:32** - "Yet now, if thou wilt forgive their sin--; and if not, blot me, I pray thee, out of thy book which thou hast written" (**KJV**).

He calls all who remained faithful to God to his side, including Aaron, and commands they kill their neighbors, friends, and brothers who forced Aaron to make the idol for them. **Exodus 32** describes the scene and claims "about three thousand people" were killed by Moses' Levites. Afterwards, God tells Moses he will not accompany the people anymore because they are "stiff-necked people" and, should he travel further with them, he would wind up killing them out of frustration.

> **Exodus 32:27-28** - "Then he said to them, 'This is what the LORD, the God of Israel, says: Each man strap a sword to his side. Go back and forth through the camp from one end to the other, each killing his brother and friend and neighbor'. The Levites did as Moses commanded, and that day about three thousand of the people died" (**NIV**).

Moses and the elders then enter into a covenant with God by which he will be their only god and they will be his chosen people. He will travel with them personally as a divine presence to direct and comfort them. God writes the Ten Commandments on new tablets which Moses cuts for him and these are placed in the ark of the covenant and the ark is housed in the tabernacle, an elaborate tent.

Even with God in their midst, however, the people still doubt and still fear and still question and so it is decreed that this generation will wander in the desert until they die; the next generation will be the one to see the promised land. Moses then leads his people through the desert for forty years until this is accomplished and the younger generation reaches the promised land of Canaan. Moses himself is not allowed to enter, only to look upon it from across the River Jordan. He dies and is buried in an unmarked grave on Mount Nebo and leadership is assumed by his second-in-command, Joshua son of Nun (Bible Study Fellowship, 2009).

The saddest event in Moses' life might well be God's prohibiting him from entering the land of Israel. The reason for this ban is explicitly connected to an episode in **Numbers** in which the Hebrews angrily demand that Moses supply them with water. God commands Moses to assemble the community, and before their very eyes order the rock to yield its water. Fed up with the Hebrews' constant whining and complaining, he says to them instead: "Listen, you rebels, shall we get water for you out of this rock?" He then strikes the rock twice with his rod, and water gushes out:

> **Numbers 20:2-13** - "Now there was no water for the community, and the people gathered in opposition to Moses and Aaron. They quarreled with Moses and said, "If only we had died when our brothers fell dead before the LORD! Why did you bring the LORD's community into this wilderness, that we and our livestock should die here? Why did you bring us up out of Egypt to this terrible place? It has no grain or figs, grapevines or pomegranates. And there is no water to drink!" Moses and Aaron went from the assembly to the entrance to the tent of meeting and fell facedown, and the glory of the LORD appeared to them. The LORD said to Moses, "Take the staff, and you and your brother Aaron gather the assembly together. Speak to that rock before their eyes and it will pour out its water. You will bring water out of the rock for the community so they and their livestock can drink." So Moses took the staff from the LORD's presence, just as he commanded him. He and Aaron gathered the assembly together in front of the rock and Moses said to them, "Listen, you rebels, must we bring

you water out of this rock?" Then Moses raised his arm and struck the rock twice with his staff. Water gushed out, and the community and their livestock drank. But the LORD said to Moses and Aaron, "Because you did not trust in me enough to honor me as holy in the sight of the Israelites, you will not bring this community into the land I give them." These were the waters of Meribah, where the Israelites quarreled with the LORD and where he was proved holy among them" **(NIV)**.

It is this episode of disobedience, striking the rock instead of speaking to it, that is generally offered as the explanation for why God punishes Moses and forbids him to enter Israel. The punishment, however, seems so disproportionate to the offense, that the real reason for God's prohibition must go deeper. Some say it was Moses' sin in declaring, "Shall we get water for you out of this rock?" Others say Moses' sin was something else altogether.

Numbers records that when ten of the twelve spies returned from Canaan and gloomily predicted that the Hebrews would never be able to conquer the land, the Israelites railed against Moses. In response, he seems to have had a mini-breakdown:

> **Numbers 14:5** - "Then Moses and Aaron fell on their faces before all the assembly of the congregation of the children of Israel" **(KJV)**.

The two independent spies, Joshua and Caleb, both of whom rejected the majority report, took over and exhorted the whole Israelite community:

> **Numbers 14:7** - "And they spake unto all the company of the children of Israel, saying, The land, which we passed through to search it, is an exceeding good land" **(KJV)**.

Later, in **Deuteronomy**, when Moses delivers his final summing-up to the Israelites, he refers back to this episode:

Deuteronomy 1:34-38 - "And the LORD heard the voice of your words, and was wroth, and sware, saying, Surely there shall not one of these men of this evil generation see that good land, which I sware to give unto your fathers. Save Caleb the son of Jephunneh; he shall see it, and to him will I give the land that he hath trodden upon, and to his children, because he hath wholly followed the LORD. Also the LORD was angry with me for your sakes, saying, Thou also shalt not go in thither. But Joshua the son of Nun, which standeth before thee, he shall go in thither: encourage him: for he shall cause Israel to inherit it" **(KJV)**.

Aaron

The Bible does not say anything about Aaron's birth, his early life, or his upbringing. It states that he married Elisheba daughter of Amminadab, of the tribe of Judah, with whom he had four sons: Nadav, Avihu, Eleazar, and Ithamar. His brother-in-law, Nahshon, was a direct ancestor of King David. Aaron is first mentioned in the Bible when God, angry that Moses was reluctant to accept the mission to free the Israelites from the Egyptian oppression, told him that Aaron was a good speaker and that he would be Moses' spokesman (Mandel, 2007).

Aaron is best known for his role in the exodus and for being the first of the Levitical, or Aaronic, priesthood. He was born to a family of Levites during Israel's enslavement in Egypt and was Moses' older brother, three years his senior:

Exodus 7:7 - "Moses was eighty years old and Aaron eighty-three when they spoke to Pharaoh" **(NIV)**.

We are first introduced to Aaron in **Exodus 4** when God tells Moses that He will send Aaron, Moses' brother, with him to free the Israelites from Pharaoh. When God spoke to Moses through a burning bush, calling him to go back to Egypt and demand that Pharaoh free the Israelites in **Exodus 3 and 4,** Moses gave reasons why he was not a good choice for the job. Moses eventually requested that God send someone else in **Exodus 4:13,** "But Moses said, "Pardon your servant, Lord. Please send someone else" **(NIV).** And **Exodus 4:14,** "Then the LORD's anger burned against Moses and he said, 'What about your brother, Aaron the Levite? I know he can speak well. He is already on his way to meet you, and he will be glad to see you'". God went on to tell Moses that Aaron would be Moses' spokesperson: (Got Questions, 2016).

> **Exodus 4:15-17** - "You shall speak to him and put words in his mouth; I will help both of you speak and will teach you what to do. He will speak to the people for you, and it will be as if he were your mouth and as if you were God to him. But take this staff in your hand so you can perform the signs with it" **(NIV).**

Aaron continued to lead with Moses during the Israelites' desert wandering, serving somewhat as his aid and spokesperson. When the Israelites grumbled against Moses and Aaron:

> **Exodus 16:2** - "In the desert the whole community grumbled against Moses and Aaron" **(NIV).**

> **Exodus 16:6-8** - "So Moses and Aaron said to all the Israelites, 'In the evening you will know that it was the LORD who brought you out of Egypt, and in the morning you will see the glory of the LORD, because he has heard your grumbling against him. Who are we, that you should grumble against us?' Moses also said, 'You will know that it was the LORD when he gives you meat to eat in the evening and all the bread you want in the morning, because he has heard your grumbling against him. Who are we? You are not grumbling against us, but against the LORD'" **(NIV).**

Exodus 16:10 - "While Aaron was speaking to the whole Israelite community, they looked toward the desert, and there was the glory of the LORD appearing in the cloud" **(NIV)**.

It was at this time that God provided quail and manna. God instructed Moses to keep an omer of manna in a jar that would be kept for generations to come. Moses asked Aaron to collect it:

Exodus 16:32-35 - "Moses said, "This is what the LORD has commanded: 'Take an omer of manna and keep it for the generations to come, so they can see the bread I gave you to eat in the wilderness when I brought you out of Egypt.'" So Moses said to Aaron, "Take a jar and put an omer of manna in it. Then place it before the LORD to be kept for the generations to come." As the LORD commanded Moses, Aaron put the manna with the tablets of the covenant law, so that it might be preserved. The Israelites ate manna forty years, until they came to a land that was settled; they ate manna until they reached the border of Canaan" **(NIV)**.

At Mount Sinai, God warned the people to keep their distance as God met with Moses and gave him the Law. On one of Moses' ascents, God told him to bring Aaron with him:

Exodus 19:24 - "The LORD replied, "Go down and bring Aaron up with you. But the priests and the people must not force their way through to come up to the LORD, or he will break out against them" **(NIV)**.

Later, when Moses stayed on the mountain with God, he put Aaron and Hur in charge to handle any disputes that might arise:

Exodus 24:14 - "He said to the elders, "Wait here for us until we come back to you. Aaron and Hur are with you, and anyone involved in a dispute can go to them" **(NIV)**.

Unfortunately, things did not go well for Aaron while he was in charge. The people became impatient waiting for Moses to return and asked Aaron to make them a god. Seemingly without resistance to the people's urge, Aaron requested their golden jewelry, formed it into the shape of a calf, and created an idol. Aaron even built an altar in front of the calf and announced a festival for it:

> **Exodus 32:1-6 -** "When the people saw that Moses was so long in coming down from the mountain, they gathered around Aaron and said, "Come, make us gods who will go before us. As for this fellow Moses who brought us up out of Egypt, we don't know what has happened to him." Aaron answered them, "Take off the gold earrings that your wives, your sons and your daughters are wearing, and bring them to me." So all the people took off their earrings and brought them to Aaron. He took what they handed him and made it into an idol cast in the shape of a calf, fashioning it with a tool. Then they said, "These are your gods, Israel, who brought you up out of Egypt." When Aaron saw this, he built an altar in front of the calf and announced, "Tomorrow there will be a festival to the LORD." So the next day the people rose early and sacrificed burnt offerings and presented fellowship offerings. Afterward they sat down to eat and drink and got up to indulge in revelry" **(NIV)**.

It may seem difficult to understand how a man who had so willingly obeyed God's call to help his brother lead the people out of Egypt, had seen God's amazing works firsthand, and just recently had seen God on Mount Sinai could do such a thing. Aaron's failure is a demonstration of our human natures. We don't know Aaron's motivation, but it is not hard to imagine that he might have doubted God and feared the people.

When God told Moses what was happening with the people and the golden calf, He threatened to destroy the people and make a great nation out of Moses instead. Moses intervened on behalf of the people and returned to them:

> **Exodus 32:7-10** - "Then the LORD said to Moses, "Go down, because your people, whom you brought up out of Egypt, have become corrupt. They have been quick to turn away from what I commanded them and have made themselves an idol cast in the shape of a calf. They have bowed down to it and sacrificed to it and have said, 'These are your gods, Israel, who brought you up out of Egypt.'"I have seen these people," the LORD said to Moses, "and they are a stiff-necked people. Now leave me alone so that my anger may burn against them and that I may destroy them. Then I will make you into a great nation" (**NIV**).

When Moses actually saw what was occurring, "his anger burned and he threw the tablets out of his hands, breaking them to pieces at the foot of the mountain":

> **Exodus 32:19** - "And it came to pass, as soon as he came nigh unto the camp, that he saw the calf, and the dancing: and Moses' anger waxed hot, and he cast the tables out of his hands, and brake them beneath the mount" (**KJV**).

The tablets contained God's covenant; it seems Moses destroyed them not just in a moment of anger, but also because the people had broken the covenant through their disobedience. Moses burned the idol, scattered its ashes in the water, and made the Israelite drink it:

> **Exodus 32:20** - "And he took the calf which they had made, and burnt it in the fire, and ground it to powder, and strawed it upon the water, and made the children of Israel drink of it" (**KJV**).

When Moses asked Aaron why the people had done this and why he'd led them into it, Aaron was honest about the people's complaining and request for him to make a god, but he was not forthcoming about his own role. Aaron admitted to his collection of their jewelry but claimed that, when he "threw it into the fire, . . . out came this calf!"

> **Exodus 32:24** - "And I said unto them, Whosoever hath any gold, let them break it off. So they gave it me: then I cast it into the fire, and there came out this calf" **(KJV)**.

Moses saw that the people were running wild and that Aaron had let them get out of control and so become a laughingstock to their enemies. Moses called those who were for the Lord to him. The Levites rallied to him, and then Moses instructed them to kill some of the people. Moses, again, interceded for the people. God reassured Moses but also sent a plague on the people for their sin:

> **Exodus 32:33-35** - "And the LORD said unto Moses, Whosoever hath sinned against me, him will I blot out of my book. Therefore now go, lead the people unto the place of which I have spoken unto thee: behold, mine Angel shall go before thee: nevertheless in the day when I visit I will visit their sin upon them. And the LORD plagued the people, because they made the calf, which Aaron made" **(KJV)**.

Aaron and his sons were appointed by God to be priests for the people, and Aaron was the first high priest. God gave Moses commandments about the priesthood, including how to consecrate priests and what garments they should wear, on Mount Sinai. God told Moses that the priesthood would belong to Aaron and his descendants by lasting ordinance:

> **Exodus 29:9** - "And thou shalt gird them with girdles, Aaron and his sons, and put the bonnets on them: and the

priest's office shall be theirs for a perpetual statute: and
thou shalt consecrate Aaron and his sons" (**KJV**).

Aaron was made the high priest, and his family line continued to serve as priests until the destruction of the temple in AD 70. The New Testament book of Hebrews spends much time comparing Jesus' permanent priesthood to the Aaronic priesthood. For instance, priests of the Levitical line had to offer sacrifices for their own sins and sacrifices on behalf of the people continually. Jesus, however, was without sin, and His sacrifice on behalf of the people was made once and was finished (**Hebrews Chapters 4-10**).

God reproved Moses and Aaron, saying, "Because you did not trust Me enough to affirm My sanctity in the sight of the Israelite people, therefore you shall not lead this congregation into the land which I have given them:

> **Numbers 20:12** - "But the LORD said to Moses and Aaron, "Because you did not trust in me enough to honor me as holy in the sight of the Israelites, you will not bring this community into the land I give them" (**NIV**).

Thus Aaron never lived to see the Promised Land. He died on Mount Hor, near the southern end of the Dead Sea when he was 123 years old. The Israelite mourned him for 30 days, the same number of days that they mourned when, some time later, Moses died. Aaron was succeeded as High Priest by his son Eleazar.

Aaron's life is a demonstration of God's holiness and His grace. Aaron began as an obedient and faithful servant, willingly going to Moses and serving as an intermediary. He also faithfully served as a priest in the sacrificial system God used as a picture for His ultimate plan of salvation in Jesus Christ. Like any other human, Aaron was a sinner. After having seen God's mighty work, he still made the golden calf and led the people in worshipping it. But Aaron seems to have learned and grown, admitting his sin in speaking against Moses and accepting the deaths of his unfaithful sons. From Aaron we learn about serving others, sharing in the responsibility of leadership, and submitting to God.

The partnership of Moses and Aaron is one of the greatest examples of two companions working together to do something great. God supernaturally knitted their spirits together for the leadership role that God had for them leading the Israel people. Thus, is my premise of Spirit to Spirit. God created marriage to show the world an example of His character, to display His love in the form of the bond between two human beings. Other unions do the same. God sometimes blesses us with friends or relatives who complement us perfectly and who help us achieve more than we ever could alone. Sometimes we receive that companion and sometimes we are called to be that companion. When we listen to that call, we may become a great blessing to someone else.

God sometimes blesses us with friends who complement us perfectly, who help us achieve more than we ever could alone.

---- ❧ ----

CHAPTER 7

Spirit to Spirit

(Intuitiveness)

To be created in the image of God, means that we have been designed on a different scale than the plant or animal kingdoms.

> **Genesis 1:27** - "God created man in His own image, in the image of God He created him; male and female He created them" (**NASB**).

We have a spirit. We can discern right and wrong. We have a conscience that bothers us when we choose wrongly. And we have intuitive suspicions about things we know very little about. Some people are naturally more intuitive than others, but we can all develop this gift to some extent by simply tuning in to it.

A woman meeting a man for the first time may have an intuitive feeling that he is dishonest and lustful, even though nothing in their exchange gave that away. When she acts upon that intuition and it is proved correct, she can strengthen it by intentionally tuning in to it more often and heeding its warnings. A man may be prepared for a business merger, but intuition tells him there is more to the story, so he puts it on hold only to learn he was right. And he is very thankful he paid attention to his intuition.

The Bible recognizes that there is a spiritual realm we can interact with, and there are spiritual **forces** of evil against which we must fight:

> **Ephesians 6:12** - "For our struggle is not against flesh and blood, but against the rulers, against the powers, against the

world forces of this darkness, against the spiritual forces of wickedness in the heavenly places" (**NASB**).

But God's people are warned against seeking wisdom or participating in spiritual activity apart from GOD.

Leviticus 19:31 - "Do not turn to mediums or spiritists; do not seek them out to be defiled by them. I am the Lord your God" (**NIV**).

Leviticus 20:27 - "Now a man or a woman who is a medium or a spiritist shall surely be put to death. They shall be stoned with stones, their blood guiltiness is upon them" (**NIV**).

The Holy Spirit of God provides guidance, convicts of sin, and brings comfort to the Christian's heart and mind.

Romans 8:9-11 - "However, you are not in the flesh but in the Spirit, if indeed the Spirit of God dwells in you. But if anyone does not have the Spirit of Christ, he does not belong to Him. If Christ is in you, though the body is dead because of sin, yet the spirit is alive because of righteousness. But if the Spirit of Him who raised Jesus from the dead dwells in you, He who raised Christ Jesus from the dead will also give life to your mortal bodies through His Spirit who dwells in you" (**NASB**).

John 16:13 - "But when He, the Spirit of truth, comes, He will guide you into all the truth; for He will not speak on His own initiative, but whatever He hears, He will speak; and He will disclose to you what is to come" (**NASB**).

This is not Extra Sensory Perception (ESP), but the presence of God within us. The believer's connection with God should not be confused with human psychic ability.

If ESP could be proved by science beyond a shadow of a doubt, we could still be assured that such a thing would not be of God but rather from demonic forces:

> **II Corinthians 11:13-15** - "For such people are false apostles, deceitful workers, masquerading as apostles of Christ. And no wonder, for Satan himself masquerades as an angel of light. It is not surprising, then, if his servants also masquerade as servants of righteousness. Their end will be what their actions deserve" **(NIV)**.

To claim ESP ability is foolishness and a rejection of God's ultimate power and authority.

> **II Chronicles 33:6** - "For such people are false apostles, deceitful workers, masquerading as apostles of Christ. And no wonder, for Satan himself masquerades as an angel of light. It is not surprising, then, if his servants also masquerade as servants of righteousness. Their end will be what their actions deserve" **(NIV)**.

Demons are real, and they are liars by nature:

> **I Timothy 4:1** - "The Spirit clearly says that in later times some will abandon the faith and follow deceiving spirits and things taught by demons" **(NIV)**.

Christians must be on their guard against being led astray by bogus wisdom, false ideas, and deceptive visions. ESP, intuition, emotional impressions, or voices in one's head are no replacement for God's Word. We must reject all that downplays God's special revelation in the Bible:

> **I Peter 5:8** - "Be alert and of sober mind. Your enemy the devil prowls around like a roaring lion looking for someone to devour" **(NIV)**.

II Timothy 3:16-17 - "All Scripture is God-breathed and is useful for teaching, rebuking, correcting and training in righteousness, so that the servant of God may be thoroughly equipped for every good work" (**NIV**).

Instead of relying on mystical, psychic powers such as ESP, Christians should always rely on God's wisdom and power:

Isaiah 8:19-20 - "When someone tells you to consult mediums and spiritists, who whisper and mutter, should not a people inquire of their God? Why consult the dead on behalf of the living? Consult God's instruction and the testimony of warning. If anyone does not speak according to this word, they have no light of dawn" (**NIV**).

James 1:5 - "If any of you lacks wisdom, you should ask God, who gives generously to all without finding fault, and it will be given to you" (**NIV**).

Psalm 28:7 - "The LORD is my strength and my shield; my heart trusts in him, and he helps me. My heart leaps for joy, and with my song I praise him" (**NIV**).

God has spoken, and He has spoken clearly:

Micah 6:8 - "He has shown you, O mortal, what is good. And what does the LORD require of you? To act justly and to love mercy and to walk humbly with your God."

Psalm 119:18 - "Open my eyes that I may see wonderful things in your law" (**NIV**).

The perception we need is only "extrasensory" in the sense that it comes from God, and the goal of having perception is to understand the eternal, unchanging, written Word of God.

Believers should not try to develop their ESP "skills" or hunger for mystical knowledge apart from what God has granted in His Word. We are to develop Christ likeness and hunger for righteousness.

> **Matthew 5:6** - "Blessed are those who hunger and thirst for righteousness, for they will be filled" **(NIV)**.

We must strive to become good servants of the Lord, having nothing to do with irreverent, selfish, or occult practices. We must train ourselves for godliness through obedience to Christ, because godliness benefits both the present life and the eternal life to come:

> **I Timothy 4:7-8** - "Have nothing to do with godless myths and old wives' tales; rather, train yourself to be godly. For physical training is of some value, but godliness has value for all things, holding promise for both the present life and the life to come" **(NIV)**.

> **James 4:7** - "Submit yourselves, then, to God. Resist the devil, and he will flee from you" **(NIV)**.

However, one's feelings can be wrong, and not all inner leanings should be heeded.

> **Proverbs 16:25** - "There is a way that appears to be right, but in the end it leads to death" **(NIV)**.

> **Ephesians 6:16** - "In addition to all this, take up the shield of faith, with which you can extinguish all the flaming arrows of the evil one" **(NIV)**.

A life not surrendered to the lordship of Jesus is easy prey for Satan's suggestions. What may feel like intuition can just as easily be one of the enemy's "fiery arrows". Because of our sinful nature, we are prone to error and poor judgment. If relying only upon our own powers of discernment, we can be led astray.

For a Christian, intuition can only be enhanced by the Holy Spirit. He is the fountain of wisdom and understanding. Those who "walk in the Spirit" have the privilege of God's own perspective on many life decisions as He guides us through His Word. We can fine tune this ability to hear God by spending time in His Word, in worship, and in meditation.

> **Galatians 5:16** - "So I say, walk by the Spirit, and you will not gratify the desires of the flesh" **(NIV)**.

> **Galatians 5:25** - "Since we live by the Spirit, let us keep in step with the Spirit" **(NIV)**.

> **I Thessalonians 3:13** - "May he strengthen your hearts so that you will be blameless and holy in the presence of our God and Father when our Lord Jesus comes with all his holy ones" **(NIV)**.

> **Job 1:1** - "In the land of Uz there lived a man whose name was Job. This man was blameless and upright; he feared God and shunned evil" **(NIV)**.

David "sat before the Lord" enjoying His presence and quieting his spirit. Our spirits hear God when we quiet our minds enough to meditate on His Word.

> **II Samuel 7:18** - "Then King David went in and sat before the LORD, and he said: 'Who am I,
>
> Sovereign LORD, and what is my family, that you have brought me this far'" **(NIV)**?

As we seek God's guidance and pray for direction, He says to trust that we have the wisdom we've asked for:

James 1:5 - "If any of you lacks wisdom, you should ask God, who gives generously to all without finding fault, and it will be given to you" (**NIV**).

Heeding our God-given intuition, we move forward in the way that seems wisest, trusting that the Lord is directing our steps:

Psalm 37:23 - "The LORD makes firm the steps of the one who delights in him" (**NIV**).

When intuition is rooted in God's Word, surrendered to the control of the Holy Spirit, and aligned with God's wisdom, it will protect us from errors and help keep our feet on the straight path:

Proverbs 4:26 - "Give careful thought to the paths for your feet and be steadfast in all your ways" (**NLT**).

Proverbs 15:21 - "Folly brings joy to one who has no sense, but whoever has understanding keeps a straight course" (**NIV**).

Isaiah 26:7 - "The path of the righteous is level; you, the Upright One, make the way of the righteous smooth" (**NLT**).

"I had a feeling that was going to happen". We've all said that at some point about an event or a person. Intuition is the feeling that causes us to know certain things without fully understanding how or why. We experience strong inner leanings toward or away from people, situations, or future decisions that we cannot explain, and many times, in the experience of the wise, those leanings prove to be correct. Intuition is a gift from God, and when we learn how to accept, develop and strengthen it, intuition can help us steer clear of disastrous decisions and relationships (Got Questions, 2019).

Your Inner Voice

Studies and evidence reveal that our intuition or gut feelings are correct an astonishing 80% of the time. How often have you thought something and then decided on the next step based on logical thinking, instead of your gut feeling? So many of us kick ourselves when we have acted in a contradictory way, and indeed our intuition is proved right. Our instinct is an inner voice, often flagging up an intuitive sense that may feel like just a strong 'knowing' or a feeling of suspicion against what our brains are telling us. Our intuition if you like, bridges a gap between logical thinking, instinct and reason, between the unconscious mind and the conscious.

What is Intuition?

> **Job 38:36** - "Who gives intuition to the heart and instinct to the mind" (**NLT**)?

Intuition is the ability to understand or know something without conscious reasoning. It is similar to an insight that we have regarding a matter. For instance, have you felt as if something is not right, or that something bad is about to happen without having any concrete facts? This is due to our intuition. We do not have real facts or a rationale for our feeling, but we feel as if it is correct. When intuition comes to play, we do not analyze the situation. We also do not weigh the pros and cons, we just know. For instance, before arriving at a decision, people approach it in different angles. They try to work out the best manner of doing something, verifying the advantages and disadvantages.

However, with intuition, one does not have sufficient information to rationalize his decision, or thought. It is as if the individual can see beyond what is presented. Intuition is like the north star of the human soul - an ever-present inner guide that helps us navigate the different landscapes of life. It's that impossible inner knowing, that soft spiritual nudge, telling you to go this way, read that book, speak to these people, or follow that road.

After a believer has embarked on a spiritual life, his spirit's senses and functions grow and fully develop. Before a believer's spirit is separated from the soul and joined to the Lord as one spirit, it is hard for him to notice the senses in his spirit. But once the power of the Holy Spirit is poured into his spirit and his inner man is strengthened, his spirit will possess the senses and functions of a full-grown man. Only then will he be able to understand the various senses of his spirit.

This sense of the spirit is called the intuition because it comes without any cause or reason. It comes "intuitively" without passing through any means. Our ordinary senses are aroused by specific means, which may be people, things, or events. These things give rise to certain feelings. If there is something to rejoice about, we rejoice. If there is something to be sorrowful about, we feel sorrow. All these senses are aroused by something; therefore, they cannot be called intuition. The sense of the spirit does not come from any means but comes directly from our inner being.

The soul and the spirit are quite similar. Believers should not follow their soul, which means that they should not follow their thoughts, feelings, or preferences. These are all from the soul. God's way for believers is to walk according to the spirit. All other ways belong to the old creation and have no spiritual value at all. How, then, can we walk according to the spirit? Walking according to the spirit is walking according to the intuition in the spirit; this is because the intuition of the spirit expresses the thought of the spirit and of God (Bates, 2017).

Intuition – The Human Sixth Sense

Intuition is a human's sixth sense, an instinctive awareness that gives us a hunch or a gut feeling about someone or something. Animals are born with instinct that keeps them safe, to ward off predators and gives them a natural knowledge in their environment that helps them survive. Humans are born with the same instinct, only our modernized way of living, social conditioning and the constant battle between our head and our heart, means we usually make decisions based on logical reasoning (Bates, 2017).

Your intuition has always been a part of you. Whether you consciously use it or not, you rely on it to some degree in your everyday life. In business, in relationships, in your own body, in making decisions, you give credence to the voice of your Spirit. You know when you do not listen to it. You know when you should have. It may be time to address it head on, get to really know and understand it, and let it truly work with you. Developing your intuition gives you that option and ultimately that power (Hausauer, 2019).

We all have it, "Intuition", "The gut feeling", "The voice in your ear, and in your soul." Some of us choose to ignore it, and others chase it. We have the option of shushing the noises we hear, or living vicariously through them. In the past, when my gut tells me to do something, I listen. Through my years of experience, years of abusing my inner voice and years of stresses, I GET IT! I feel as though I have learned many, many lessons, and now I know the choices I need to make in order to move forward (Hausauer, 2019). My prayer is that you will, too.

God's people are warned against seeking wisdom or participating in spiritual activity apart from GOD.

CHAPTER 8

Testing the Spirits

Satan is the god of this world, the prince of the power of the air, the ruler of spiritual darkness in heavenly places, and he has been allowed to run loose in this world, going about as a roaring lion, seeking who he may devour. He and his agents are disguised as angels of light, according to the apostle Paul in his letter to the Corinthians. And we should not be surprised that Satan operates 99 percent of the time in false religion, in lies and deception (MacArthur, 2013).

When Satan fell he took a third of the other angels with him. Satan in the Bible has many names. He is called ruler of the world, God of this world, adversary, The Devil, murderer, liar, father of both, angel of the abyss, serpent, and tempter. The angels who fell with him are called demons and angels. Now that these angels are no longer in heaven, no longer serving God, what then do they do? They now serve Satan and spend their existence trying to destroy God's creation. How do they do this?

By pretending to be God's angels, by disguising themselves as angels of light to deceive men and lead them astray from God and the truth:

> **II Corinthians 11:14** - "And no wonder! Even Satan disguises himself as an angel of light" (**RVS**).

Being that this is true, how then do we distinguish from an angel of God, a spirit from God, and an angel from Satan pretending to be God's messenger? If you receive an impression or a spirit appears to you as an angel of light claiming to have a message from God, The Bible tells us that we are to test that spirit to see if it is from God. John wrote in:

> **I John 4:1-3** - "Beloved, do not believe every spirit, but test the spirits to see whether they are from God; for many false prophets have gone out into the world. By this you know the Spirit of God: every spirit that confesses that Jesus Christ has come in the flesh is from God, and every spirit that does not confess Jesus is not from God. And this is the spirit of the Antichrist, of which you have heard that it is coming; and now it is already in the world" **(RSV).**

Therefore, it is very important that you know how to test the spirits, to know whether they are from God or not. A spirit may manifest itself to you in various ways, to include the following:

- It may appear to you directly;
- It may appear to you in a dream;
- It may whisper a thought in your ear;
- It may resemble a person you know or may look like an angel of light!

To test a spirit, the Bible says that you need to ask it a question. Read **I John 4** carefully:

> **I John 4:1-6** - "Dear friends, do not believe every spirit, but test the spirits to see whether they are from God, because many false prophets have gone out into the world. This is how you can recognize the Spirit of God: Every spirit that acknowledges that Jesus Christ has come in the flesh is from God, but every spirit that does not acknowledge Jesus is not from God. This is the spirit of the Antichrist, which you have heard is coming and even now is already in the world. You, dear children, are from God and have overcome them, because the one who is in you is greater than the one who is in the world. They are from the world and therefore speak from the viewpoint of the world, and the world listens to them. We are from God, and whoever knows God listens

to us; but whoever is not from God does not listen to us. This is how we recognize the Spirit of truth and the spirit of falsehood" (**RSV**).

What's the question you should ask every spirit? Simply this:

Ask every spirit to confess that Jesus Christ is come in the flesh.

If that spirit is from God, it will confess that Jesus Christ is come in the flesh. If it's not from God, it will not. But no matter what response I sense or hear, if that response is not a "Yes, Jesus Christ is come in the flesh!" then I know that spirit is from the wicked one. I immediately command it to leave me in Jesus' name.

> **James 2:19** says, "You believe that there is one God. Good! Even the demons believe that and shudder" (**RSV**).

So don't let an enemy spirit wiggle its way around the question or avoid the question. Make it clear, and make it specific and listen carefully for the answer. Any spirit that comes to you MUST confess specifically that Jesus Christ is come in the flesh in order to be from God. You can, and should, also ask God to give you the gift of discernment of spirits. This gift will NOT take away the need for you to ask EVERY spirit to confess that Jesus Christ is come in the flesh. However, it does make it a whole lot easier to distinguish between the holy voices of God and His angels/ministers, and the evil voices of the enemy and his minions (Rohrbaugh, 2017).

> **Matthew 24:24** - "For false messiahs and false prophets will appear and perform great signs and wonders to deceive, if possible, even the elect" (**NIV**).

I knew of testing spirits and I had seen it done before. But I had become too confident in my own abilities and could not see that I also could be deceived, so I began testing spirits when I would pray for God's will or for His discernment. If I was praying about something pretty big, I would always pray to make sure I was hearing from God. We must be very aware because even Peter, who had a close relationship with Jesus, was led astray by the lies of Satan.

It is possible for any person to be deceived by false prophets and lies of the devil. We know that the devil disguises himself as an angel of light, posing as something good and attempting to lure us away from God's truth. That is exactly the way he seduced Adam and Eve. The devil has been around for a very long time. He knows the weaknesses of human beings and puts a lot of hours into finding out each person's weakness. And because he knows the call each of us has on our lives, he knows how to get to us so he can steal that from us. The devil is a liar, and a wolf in sheep's clothing. So, testing spirits is not only scriptural, but critical to protect and develop our relationship with God.

According to **I John:**

> **1 John 4:2-3** - "This is how you can recognize the Spirit of God: Every spirit that acknowledges that Jesus Christ has come in the flesh is from God, but every spirit that does not acknowledge Jesus is not from God. This is the spirit of the Antichrist, which you have heard is coming and even now is already in the world" (**NIV**).

So when you are seeking after the Lord for His wisdom and guidance and you hear an answer, you can ask the voice some questions. You want to make sure that this answer is coming from the Most High, so obviously if you are hearing the Holy Spirit, it will confess that Jesus Christ is Lord. Here are some questions to ask: Is this a false prophet? Do you confess Jesus Christ is the son of the Living God?

As you are listening for an answer, remember that God will never answer inconsistently with His character or nature. As you are learning to distinguish His voice from others, be sure to compare your answer with scripture. God does not change who He is, and His word will always remain a strong testament to His character and nature. And any answer from God is going to bear the fruit of the Spirit with it. Therefore, if the things you are hearing don't produce love, joy, peace, forbearance, kindness, goodness, faithfulness, gentleness and self control in you or those around you, then that is not the voice of God.

You can also take your question and answer to a reliable person who is strong in their relationship with the Lord for an outside opinion. But in the end, you must never rely on others for advice, because it could dampen your own growth in your discernment for the Lord. If you are able to hear the Lord in prayer, then you can hear answers to these questions. If you are hearing answers to these questions that don't line up with Jesus Christ being the Son of God, then you know it is not Him. If you feel strongly you are up against a false prophet, then simply ask angels of the Lord to remove them from your presence, or tell the spirit that it needs to loose and leave you, in Jesus Name.

Every single person has the ability to hear the voice of God. If you are struggling to hear the voice of the Lord, there are many reasons that might be a problem. The first step is to just seek Him with all of your heart and soul and mind, developing a closeness with Him. You must trust that no matter what you feel, He is there, His presence is available, that He loves you, and He has never left you. I know many people do struggle with this issue, and I will continue to teach about it (Moore, 2016).

I want to be clear, that while the process of testing the spirits is very simple, it is a process of them astray from God and the truth:

II Corinthians 11:14 - "And no wonder! Even Satan disguises himself as an angel of light" **(RVS)**.

Being that this is true, how then do we distinguish from an angel of God, a spirit from God, and an angel from Satan pretending to be God's messenger? If you receive an impression or a spirit appears to you as an angel of light claiming to have a message from God, The Bible tells us that we are to test that spirit to see if it is from God. John wrote in:

> **I John 4:1-3** - "Beloved, do not believe every spirit, but test the spirits to see whether they are from God; for many false prophets have gone out into the world. By this you know the Spirit of God: every spirit that confesses that Jesus Christ has come in the flesh is from God, and every spirit that does not confess Jesus is not from God. And this is the spirit of the Antichrist, of which you have heard that it is coming; and now it is already in the world" **(RSV)**.

What exactly does it mean to test the spirits? According to the Bible, we need to test every spirit that comes to us to see whether it is from God or not. When the Bible says spirit, it means the spirit of a man and the spirits that come through man. We will come into contact with Christians who are aligned with darkness purposefully, and are set to deceive us; but we will also come into contact with Christians who have aligned with darkness and have no idea. It is through the darkness within them that they will attempt to deceive us, because there are evil spirits that are using them for this purpose.

When people have areas of themselves they have given over to darkness, this does not mean they are evil or bad. It means they have been deceived and have given over the truth for a lie. It happens to everyone at some point, and we cannot judge others by their actions, but only by the spirit. It is our job to continue to surrender our hearts to God, and work towards letting more and more of His Spirit into our persons. It is through this submission that we can be in alignment with God and His will for our lives.

We need to test every spirit that comes to us!

CHAPTER 9

He Touched Me

Humans are made with a need to belong, and appropriate physical contact with other people is critical to our sense of relationship and well being. Studies have shown the negative effects of a lack of safe touch, which range from developmental and emotional issues to an increased susceptibility to disease (Maheson. 2019).

> **Luke 8:46** - "But Jesus said, "Someone touched me; I know that power has gone out from me" (**NIV**).

In **Leviticus**, the Israelites were wandering in the desert after 400 years of captivity in Egypt trying to gain a sense of their national identity. More than anything, they needed to know that they were supposed to be different than the surrounding nations, set apart for their God. So God directed Moses to lay out a detailed set of rules for the Israelites governing everything from worship practices to healthcare. By the time Jesus arrived on the scene, over a thousand years of tradition had shaped the culture, dividing nearly everything and everyone into categories of "clean" and "unclean."

Jesus studied the law. He knew the command in:

> **Leviticus 13:45-46** - "Those who suffer from a serious skin disease must tear their clothing and leave their hair uncombed. They must cover their mouth and call out, 'Unclean! Unclean!'. As long as the serious disease lasts, they will be ceremonially unclean. They must live in isolation in their place outside the camp" (**NLT**).

People with serious skin conditions had to tear their clothing, leave their hair uncombed, call out to warn people of their approach and "live in isolation outside the camp."

And he also knew that contact with anyone "unclean" would ceremonially contaminate him too, preventing him from participating in worship at the temple for a time. Jesus understood that people expected him to avoid those they believed didn't belong. Near the beginning of his public ministry, Jesus had an encounter with someone that must have raised some eyebrows:

> **Luke 5:12-13** - "In one of the villages, Jesus met a man with an advanced case of leprosy. When the man saw Jesus, he bowed with his face to the ground, begging to be healed. 'Lord,' he said, 'if you are willing, you can heal me and make me clean.' Jesus reached out and touched him. 'I am willing,' he said. 'Be healed!' And instantly the leprosy disappeared" (**NLT**).

The man's agony was obvious as he laid face-first on the ground, not just physical pain, but emotional as well. The man said, "If you are willing" (emphasis mine). He didn't assume Jesus would want to help him; after all, this man was a leper, an outcast and a risk to everyone around him.

Jesus could have simply spoken aloud and healed the man's leprosy, restoring the his health and place in the community. Instead, Jesus laid his hand on the man while his skin was still diseased, accepting him while he was still a leper.

Jesus was also aware of this commandment:

> **Leviticus 15:25** - "If a woman has a flow of blood for many days that is unrelated to her menstrual period, or if the blood continues beyond the normal period, she is ceremonially unclean. As during her menstrual period, the woman will be unclean as long as the discharge continues" (**NLT**).

Just a few chapters later in Luke, Jesus once again pushed social boundaries in his response to a woman:

> **Luke 8:43-48** - "A woman in the crowd had suffered for twelve years with constant bleeding, and she could find no cure. Coming up behind Jesus, she touched the fringe of his robe. Immediately, the bleeding stopped. "Who touched me?" Jesus asked. Everyone denied it, and Peter said, "Master, this whole crowd is pressing up against you." But Jesus said, "Someone deliberately touched me, for I felt healing power go out from me." When the woman realized that she could not stay hidden, she began to tremble and fell to her knees in front of him. The whole crowd heard her explain why she had touched him and that she had been immediately healed. "Daughter," he said to her, "your faith has made you well. Go in peace" (**NLT**).

After 12 years of suffering and isolation, the woman was desperate for healing, desperate enough to take an enormous social risk. She touched the fringe along the edge of the hem of Jesus' robe, which wasn't just for decoration; in Hebrew tradition, that fringe served as a visible reminder of God's law.

> **Numbers 15:39** - "When you see the tassels, you will remember and obey all the commands of the LORD instead of following your own desires and defiling yourselves, as you are prone to do" (**NLT**).

A normal man likely would have been angry that she contaminated the holy edge of his robe. He might have made a scene, demanding her punishment and humiliating her even further than her condition already had.

What must she have been feeling when Jesus stopped and asked, "Who touched me?" Jesus could have let her healing remain a secret, allowing her to slide quietly back into regular life and relationships. Instead, he listened to her story and then gently called her "daughter," communicating two astonishing truths to everyone: Jesus couldn't be contaminated, because he was the source of cleansing and wholeness, and he tenderly welcomed her brazen act of faith.

Jesus' interactions with the man with leprosy and the bleeding woman reached beyond their physical ailments to their deeper pain and longing. The Lord, who left a series of miracles in HIS wake, valued them enough to pause just for them. He stood and intentionally touched the leper. He stayed and compassionately received the touch of the bleeding woman. These are examples of the human experience of touch and in these cases JESUS touched them and they were forever changed and healed.

Therefore, back to my premise and foundation of touch, it is the deepest of all touches.

JESUS touched them and they were forever changed!

CHAPTER 10

Worship Him in Spirit

"For God is Spirit, so those who worship him must worship in spirit and in truth."
John 4:24
(NLT)

Worshipping God "in spirit" means with reverence, attentiveness, and having the right purpose of honoring God, while understanding what we are doing. Our worship must glorify God.

> **I Corinthians 6:20** says, "For you were bought with a price; therefore glorify God in your body and in your spirit, which are God's" **(KJV)**.

A proper foundation of our worship depends on our motivation. If we are motivated by what appeals solely to our lustful desires then our worship will not be pleasing to God.

> **I John 2:15-16** - "Love not the world, neither the things that are in the world. If any man love the world, the love of the Father is not in him. For all that is in the world, the lust of the flesh, and the lust of the eyes, and the pride of life, is not of the Father, but is of the world" **(KJV)**.

However, if our worship is based on our love for God because of what He did by sending His Son Jesus to die on the cross for our sins; it is pleasing to Him:

> **Isaiah 56:6-7** - "Also the sons of the stranger, that join themselves to the LORD, to serve him, and to love the name

of the LORD, to be his servants, every one that keepeth the sabbath from polluting it, and taketh hold of my covenant; Even them will I bring to my holy mountain, and make them joyful in my house of prayer: their burnt offerings and their sacrifices shall be accepted upon mine altar; for mine house shall be called an house of prayer for all people" **(KJV)**.

II Corinthians 5:5-9 - "Now he that hath wrought us for the selfsame thing is God, who also hath given unto us the earnest of the Spirit. Therefore we are always confident, knowing that, whilst we are at home in the body, we are absent from the Lord: (For we walk by faith, not by sight:) We are confident, I say, and willing rather to be absent from the body, and to be present with the Lord. Wherefore we labour, that, whether present or absent, we may be accepted of him" **(KJV)**.

With the proper foundation, we can then focus on what it means to worship in Spirit. As Piper writes, "True worship comes only from spirits made alive and sensitive by the quickening of the Spirit of God. God's Spirit ignites and energizes our spirit" (Piper, 2011). If God is spirit then he can't be confined to a building, an icon or any other thing. If God is spirit and not confined by anything we can make, then he can be worshipped anywhere and everywhere. The early Christian saints in this land understood that, and their worship encompassed their working day as well as their leisure and devotional life. They felt the presence of God in the ordinary places that they inhabited, and in the fields in which they laboured and among the people whom they served (Birch, 2016).

The Bible says that they who worship God are to worship him "in spirit." No longer with the visible sacrifice of a lamb, but inwardly trusting in him who IS the Lamb of God; no more with sprinkled blood of goats, but relying upon HIS blood once shed for many. We no longer worship God with our many encumbrances but with a prostrate soul and an uplifted faith, and not with the faculties of the human body but with the inward spirit HE gives us. We come to understand in our worship of God that bodily exercise in worship profiteth nothing. What is acceptable worship is wholly mental, inward, and spiritual (Williams, 2014).

Another crucial verse concerning the human spirit is:

> **II Timothy 4:22** - "May the Lord be with your spirit. And may his grace be with all of you" (**NLT**).

This verse does not say that the Lord is with our mind or soul or heart; it tells us that He is with our spirit. Deep within, in the center of our being, we have a particular being, the human spirit, created by God for the purpose of receiving Him and containing Him. Our regenerated human spirit matches Christ, who is the Spirit:

> **II Corinthians 3:17** - **"For the Lord is the Spirit, and wherever the Spirit of the Lord is, there is freedom"** (**NLT**).

I believe that worship in spirit is, in part, emotional or felt. This is not to say that we should necessarily pump up our emotions with music or crowd fervor. Of course, worshipping the Lord is often accompanied by musical instruments and singing. It can certainly add an element of praise that will remind us that the Lord is Saviour and we owe all to Him. Genuine emotions for God stem from focusing our minds on the truth of who He is and what He has done for us at the cross. But if your worship never touches your emotions, something is wrong.

It's who you are and the way you live that count before God. Your worship must engage your spirit in the pursuit of truth. Our heavenly Father is looking for those who are simple and honest before Him in their worship. Worship is about a relationship when our spirit, our heart and soul, and that invisible and mysterious part of us that makes us who we are connect with God himself. It's so much more than just meeting together in a certain building on a Sunday, as Jesus was so keen to point out to a Samaritan woman 2000 years ago (Birch, 2016).

> **John 4:21-24** - "Jesus replied, "Believe me, dear woman, the time is coming when it will no longer matter whether you worship the Father on this mountain or in Jerusalem. You Samaritans know very little about the one you worship, while we Jews know all about him, for salvation comes through the Jews. But the time is coming—indeed it's here now—when true worshipers will worship the Father in spirit and in truth. The Father is looking for those who will worship him that way. For God is Spirit, so those who worship him must worship in spirit and in truth" (**NLT**).

Spiritual worship, rooted in the truth of God's Word, continues out of the chapel or church door and into the street and neighborhood. It continues in the way that lives are led and love is shared, because that's the way that people connect with our God. As we worship in spirit and truth, then we witness through our lives to the wonder, majesty and love of the God whom we serve; it's like the Living Water that Jesus speaks of, it flows through our worship and overflows into all areas of our lives. That's the worship that our heavenly Father wants!

To walk in the Spirit, you first need to receive the Spirit. The Spirit we are talking about here is the Holy Spirit. The Holy Spirit is a real force. When you receive this power in your life, a new day begins; it is the start of a new and immensely satisfying chapter of your life.

> **Acts 1:8** - "But ye shall receive power, after that the Holy Ghost is come upon you: and ye shall be witnesses unto me both in Jerusalem, and in all Judaea, and in Samaria, and unto the uttermost part of the earth" (**KJV**).

To walk in the Spirit means being obedient when the Spirit prompts your spirit to do the will of God.

Walking in the Spirit is life-changing.

Walking in the Spirit means being obedient to the Spirit and to the laws and commandments which the Spirit brings to your remembrance when temptations come. Being tempted is not the same as sinning, but when tempted you come to a point of decision. When someone says something spiteful or rude to you, everyone knows what sorts of temptations arise: to retaliate or get even in one way or another. If you do that you break God's commandments and that is sinning. But what does the Holy Spirit say? If you walk in this Spirit, you overcome temptation. You resolve the situation in a positive way, which gives you joy instead of releasing a destructive domino effect.

By walking in the Spirit, something incredible happens. What the Bible calls "fruits of the Spirit" begin to grow in your life:

> **Galatians 5:22** - "But the fruit of the Spirit is love, joy, peace, longsuffering, gentleness, goodness, faith, Meekness, temperance: against such there is no law" **(KJV)**.

You who were so restless, anxious, and often unhappy, will develop a healthy outlook on life. You become more stable and learn to create peace around you. You become happy, and happiness becomes a natural part of your life. You are no longer envious of others. God's love frees your thoughts from the endless demands of your ego so you instead think about others and what might be good for them. Faithfulness becomes a part of your personality. You become trustworthy in everything you say and do. You become a new person. It is no longer accurate to say, "We are only human." Something completely new is born into your life so that you reason and reason differently than before (Kennedy, 2018).

This is the life that Jesus lived on earth and which you can live as His disciple. Walking in the Spirit takes practice. You may have a misstep, particularly at the start of your Christian walk, but you must not lose courage. The Spirit is also called the "Comforter" in one translation. He comforts us and gives us more boldness and new courage when we need it. The Spirit is with us on our walk and gives us the right nourishment when we need it, when we love the truth (Kennedy, 2018).

> In **II Timothy 1:7**, it is written, "For God has not given us a spirit of fear, but of power and of love and of a sound mind" **(KJV)**.

A "walk" in the Bible is often a metaphor for practical daily living. The Christian life is a journey, and we are to walk it out; we are to make consistent forward progress. The biblical norm for all believers is that they walk in the Spirit:

> **Galatians 5:25** - "If we live in the Spirit, let us also walk in the Spirit" **(KJV)**.

> **Romans 8:14** - "For as many as are led by the Spirit of God, they are the sons of God" **(KJV)**.

In other words, the Spirit gave us life in the new birth:

> **John 3:6** - "That which is born of the flesh is flesh; and that which is born of the Spirit is spirit" **(KJV)**.

And we must continue to live, day by day, in the Spirit.

To walk in the Spirit means that we yield to His control, we follow His lead, and we allow Him to exert His influence over us. To walk in the Spirit is the opposite of resisting Him or grieving Him:

> **Ephesians 4:30** - "And do not grieve the Holy Spirit of God, with whom you were sealed for the day of redemption" **(NIV)**.

Walking in this Spirit will yield a fulfilling life. This is not philosophy or a religious theory but it is written:

> **Galatians 5:16-18** - "So I say, walk by the Spirit, and you will not gratify the desires of the flesh. For the flesh desires what is contrary to the Spirit, and the Spirit what is contrary to the flesh. They are in conflict with each other, so that you are not to do whatever you want. But if you are led by the Spirit, you are not under the law" (**NIV**).

There are many people alive today who have experienced this, and the people around them can confirm that it is true. Being a self-proclaimed believer, and being a member of a church, a religion, or religious group will not solve your problems; but, walking in the Spirit will. It will solve your inner conflicts as well as conflicts with other people. A better life, a better offer cannot be found.

It's quite a liberating thing to be able to take your worship outside of the confines of a church sanctuary and into your Monday to Saturday life! If God is spirit then our response to him must be by offering spiritual offerings like love, devotion, obedience and service. It's the offering of ourselves as we are, not the outward show of Sunday best clothing, not the size of our offering, but what's underneath, and not only what's underneath but what's inside our hearts. God looks inside the heart to see real you and me.

Those who walk in the Spirit rely on the Holy Spirit to guide them in thought, word, and deed:

> **Romans 6:11-14** - "In the same way, count yourselves dead to sin but alive to God in Christ Jesus. Therefore do not let sin reign in your mortal body so that you obey its evil desires. Do not offer any part of yourself to sin as an instrument of wickedness, but rather offer yourselves to God as those who have been brought from death to life; and offer every part of yourself to him as an instrument

of righteousness. For sin shall no longer be your master, because you are not under the law, but under grace" (**KJV**).

A spirit-filled way of life is lived according to the rule of the gospel, as the Spirit moves us toward obedience. When we walk in the Spirit, we find that the human struggles in the world and the sinful appetites of the flesh have no more dominion over us.

Walking in the Spirit is life-changing.

References

Bates, Hannah. *Intuition – The Human Sixth Sense.* LIFESTYLE. February 10, 2017.

Bible Study Fellowship, Biblical Exegesis: Moses. March, 2009.

Birch, John. *Worship in Spirit and Truth, P & R Publishing,* 2016.

Britannica Encyclopedia. *Elijah,* Encyclopedia Britannica, Inc., Chicago, IL 2015.

Britannica Encyclopedia. *Ruth,* Encyclopedia Britannica, Inc., Chicago, IL 2015.

Brown, Lachlan. *Kindred Spirit.* Blog, November 13, 2018.

Dictionary of Biblical Imagery, Ryken, Leland, InterVarsity Press, 1998.

Got Questions Ministries. *What does the Bible say about extrasensory perception (ESP)?* February 2019.

Got Questions Ministries. What *is the Christian view of psychics/fortune tellers?* February 5, 2016

Got Questions Ministries. *Who was Aaron in the Bible?* February 4, 2015.

Ham, Ken. *Answers in Genesis.* Answers Magazine, October 1, 2012.

Hausauer, Christina. The Voices of Intuition. The Startup. March 12, 2019.

Lynch, Judi, *Knowing Kindred Spirit Connections.* July 31, 2014.

Kennedy, William. *Active Christianity. What does the Holy Spirit do for us?* Published by Brunstad Christian Church, May 18, 2018.

MacArthur, John. *Testing the Spirits.* Sermon. October 17, 2013.

Mandel, David. My Jewish Learning. *Aaron, the High Priest,* The Jewish Publication Society. December 1, 2007.

Matheson, Beth. *Touched by Jesus: Invited Into Belonging.* Wycliffe, March 28, 2019.

Merriam-Webster Dictionary. *Kindred.* Merriam-Webster, Inc. New edition 2019.

Moore, Beth, *Testing Spirits,* WordPress. July 18, 2016.

Moyer, Ginny Kubitz. *Ignatian Spirituality*. Busted Halo. Paulist Media Ministry. Loyalo Press. July 20, 2018.

Nee, Watchan and Lee Witness. *The Intuition*. Living Stream Ministry, 2014.

Pelaia, Ariela. *Biography of Ruth in the Bible*. Thought Co. Dotdash. December 24, 2018.

Piper, John. *Desiring God*. Publisher: Multnomah. January 18, 2011.

Ritenbaugh, John W. Forerunner Commentary. BibleTools.org. InterVarsity Press, 2007.

Rohrbaugh, Jamie. *Supernatural Encounters*. From His Presense Miniseries. October 5, 2017.

Slick, Matt. *How did God come into being, existence?* Christian Apologetics and Research Ministry. Nampa, ID. July 17, 2017.

The Holy Bible. *King James Version,* (KJV), New York: American Bible Society: 1999.

The Holy Bible. *The New King James,* (NKJV), Thomas Nelson Publishers. 1982.

The Holy Bible. *New American Standard Bible,* (NASB), La Habra, CA: Foundation Publications, for the Lockman Foundation, 1971.

The Holy Bible. *New International Version,* (NIV), Grand Rapids: Zondervan Publishing House, 1984.

The Holy Bible. *New Living Translation,* (NLT), Tyndale House. Foundation, 2015.

The Holy Bible. *New Revised Standard Version Bible,* (NRVS), Division of Christian Education of the National Council of the Churches of Christ in the United States of America. 1989.

Watch Tower."*Bound Together in Close Friendship*". November 13, 2018.

Wellman, Jack. *Bible Character Study on Naomi*. November 30, 2018.

Williams, Michael L. *What Does It Mean To Worship In Spirit And Truth?* 2014.

Appendix 1

INTUITION

The body has its senses, and the spirit also has its senses. The spirit dwells in the body and has a very close relationship with the body; nevertheless, it is completely different from the body. The body has various senses, but a spiritual man can detect that which is beyond his physical senses. There is another sense in the innermost part of his being which can rejoice, grieve, fear, approve, condemn, determine, and discern. These are the senses of the spirit which are distinct from the senses of the soul expressed through the body.

The senses and functions of the spirit can be seen from the following verses:

"The spirit is willing" (Matthew 26:41).

"Jesus, knowing fully in His spirit" (Mark 2:8).

"He groaned deeply in His spirit" (Mark 8:12).

"My spirit has exulted in God my Savior" (Luke 1:47).

"The true worshippers will worship the Father in spirit and truthfulness" (John 4:23).

"He...was moved with indignation in His spirit" (John 11:33).

"When Jesus had said these things, He became troubled in His spirit" (John 13:21).

"His spirit was provoked within him as he beheld that the city was full of idols" (Acts 17:16).

"This man was instructed in the way of the Lord, and being fervent in spirit" (Acts 18:25).

"Paul purposed in his spirit" (Acts 19:21).

"I am going bound in the spirit to Jerusalem" (Acts 20:22).

"Burning in spirit" (Romans 12:11).

"For who among men knows the things of man, except the spirit of man which is in him?" (I Corinthians 2:11).

"I will sing with the spirit" (I Corinthians 14:15).

"If you bless with the spirit" (I Corinthians 14:16).

"I had no rest in my spirit" (II Corinthians 2:13).

"Having the same spirit of faith" (II Corinthians 4:13).

"A spirit of wisdom and revelation" (Ephesians 1:17).

"Your love in the Spirit" (Colossians 1:8).

(Nee and Lee, 2014)

Appendix 2

Covenant Relationships

Scriptures (NASB)

II Samuel 5:3

> So all the elders of Israel came to the king at Hebron, and King David made a covenant with them before the LORD at Hebron; then they anointed David king over Israel.

I Chronicles 11:3

> So all the elders of Israel came to the king at Hebron, and David made a covenant with them in Hebron before the LORD; and they anointed David king over Israel, according to the word of the LORD through Samuel.

II Samuel 3:21

> Abner said to David, "Let me arise and go and gather all Israel to my lord the king, that they may make a covenant with you, and that you may be king over all that your soul desires." So David sent Abner away, and he went in peace.

II Kings 11:17

> Then Jehoiada made a covenant between the LORD and the king and the people, that they would be the LORD'S people, also between the king and the people

II Chronicles 23:3

Then all the assembly made a covenant with the king in the house of God. And Jehoiada said to them, "Behold, the king's son shall reign, as the LORD has spoken concerning the sons of David.

Joshua 9:15

Joshua made peace with them and made a covenant with them, to let them live; and the leaders of the congregation swore an oath to them.

I Samuel 11:1

Now Nahash the Ammonite came up and besieged Jabesh-gilead; and all the men of Jabesh said to Nahash, "Make a covenant with us and we will serve you."

I Kings 15:19-20

"Let there be a treaty between you and me, as between my father and your father. Behold, I have sent you a present of silver and gold; go, break your treaty with Baasha king of Israel so that he will withdraw from me." So Ben-hadad listened to King Asa and sent the commanders of his armies against the cities of Israel, and conquered Ijon, Dan, Abel-beth-maacah and all Chinneroth, besides all the land of Naphtali.

I Kings 20:34

Ben-hadad said to him, "The cities which my father took from your father I will restore, and you shall make streets for yourself in Damascus, as my father made in Samaria." Ahab said, "And I will let you go with this covenant." So he made a covenant with him and let him go.

Ezekiel 17:13-14

'He took one of the royal family and made a covenant with him, putting him under oath He also took away the mighty of the land, that the kingdom might be in subjection, not exalting itself, but keeping his covenant that it might continue.

I Kings 5:12

The LORD gave wisdom to Solomon, just as He promised him; and there was peace between Hiram and Solomon, and the two of them made a covenant.

Genesis 21:27

Abraham took sheep and oxen and gave them to Abimelech, and the two of them made a covenant

Genesis 26:28-29

They said, "We see plainly that the LORD has been with you; so we said, 'Let there now be an oath between us, even between you and us, and let us make a covenant with you, that you will do us no harm, just as we have not touched you and have done to you nothing but good and have sent you away in peace. You are now the blessed of the LORD.'"

Genesis 31:44

"So now come, let us make a covenant, you and I, and let it be a witness between you and me."

Amos 1:9

Thus says the LORD, "For three transgressions of Tyre and for four I will not revoke its punishment, Because they delivered up an entire population to Edom And did not remember the covenant of brotherhood.

Jeremiah 34:8

The word which came to Jeremiah from the LORD after King Zedekiah had made a covenant with all the people who were in Jerusalem to proclaim release to them:

II Kings 11:4

Now in the seventh year Jehoiada sent and brought the captains of hundreds of the Carites and of the guard, and brought them to him in the house of the LORD. Then he made a covenant with them and put them under oath in the house of the LORD, and showed them the king's son.

II Chronicles 23:1

Now in the seventh year Jehoiada strengthened himself, and took captains of hundreds: Azariah the son of Jeroham, Ishmael the son of Johanan, Azariah the son of Obed, Maaseiah the son of Adaiah, and Elishaphat the son of Zichri, and they entered into a covenant with him.

Ezra 10:3

God to put away all the wives and their children, according to the counsel of my lord and of those who tremble at the commandment of our God; and let it be done according to the law.

Nehemiah 9:38

"Now because of all this We are making an agreement in writing; And on the sealed document are the names of our leaders, our Levites and our priests."

Psalm 83:5

For they have conspired together with one mind; Against You they make a covenant:

Proverbs 2:17

That leaves the companion of her youth And forgets the covenant of her God;

Malach 2:14

"Yet you say, 'For what reason?' Because the LORD has been a witness between you and the wife of your youth, against whom you have dealt treacherously, though she is your companion and your wife by covenant.

Jeremiah 2:2

"Go and proclaim in the ears of Jerusalem, saying, 'Thus says the LORD, "I remember concerning you the devotion of your youth, The love of your betrothals, Your following after Me in the wilderness, Through a land not sown.

Ezekiel 16:8

"Then I passed by you and saw you, and behold, you were at the time for love; so I spread My skirt over you and covered your nakedness I also swore to you and entered into a covenant with you so that you became Mine," declares the Lord GOD.

I Samuel 18:3

Then Jonathan made a covenant with David because he loved him as himself.

I Samuel 20:16-17

So Jonathan made a covenant with the house of David, saying, "May the LORD require it at the hands of David's enemies." Jonathan made David vow again because of his love for him, because he loved him as he loved his own life.

The Bible uses two consistent images in its representation of friendship.

The first is that of the knitting of souls together.

Deuteronomy provides the earliest mention in this regard when it speaks of a "friend who is as your own soul":

> **Deuteronomy 13:6** - "If your very own brother, or your son or daughter, or the wife you love, or your closest friend secretly entices you, saying, "Let us go and worship other gods" (gods that neither you nor your ancestors have known)" **(NIV)**.

That is, one who is a companion of one's innermost thoughts and feelings. Prominent in this reflection on friendship is the concept of intimacy. It is well illustrated by Jonathan and David's friendship. For example, in:

> **I Samuel 18:1** - "After David had finished talking with Saul, Jonathan became one in spirit with David, and he loved him as himself" **(NIV)**.

We read that the "soul of Jonathan was knit to the soul of David, and Jonathan loved him as his own soul." This reflection on the meaning of friendship bears with it ideas of strong emotional attachment and loyalty. Not surprisingly, the term 'friend' naturally became another name for believers or brothers and sisters in the Lord:

> **III John 14** - "I hope to see you soon, and we will talk face to face. Peace to you. The friends here send their greetings. Greet the friends there by name" (**NIV**).

The second image that the Bible uses to represent friendship is the face-to-face encounter.

This is literally the image used for Moses' relationship to God. In the tabernacle God spoke to Moses 'face to face, as a man speaks to his friend'

> **Exodus 33:11** - "And the Lord spake unto Moses face to face, as a man speaketh unto his friend. And he turned again into the camp: but his servant Joshua, the son of Nun, a young man, departed not out of the tabernacle" (**NIV**).

> **Numbers 12:8** - "With him will I speak mouth to mouth, even apparently, and not in dark speeches; and the similitude of the Lord shall he behold: wherefore then were ye not afraid to speak against my servant Moses" (**NIV**)?

The face-to-face image implies a conversation, a sharing of confidences and consequently a meeting of minds, goals and direction. In the New Testament, we find a similar idea expressed in:

> **II John 12** - "Having many things to write unto you, I would not write with paper and ink: but I trust to come unto you, and speak face to face, that our joy may be full" (**NIV**).

The Elder tells his readers that he wants to speak to them "face to face." One of the benefits of such face-to-face encounters between friends is the heightened insight that such times of friendship produce. As the famous saying in:

> **Proverbs 27:17** - "As iron sharpens iron, so one person sharpens another" (**NIV**).

The Dictionary of Biblical Imagery comments: Friendship entails responsibilities and benefits. The proverb that "a friend loves at all times".

> **Proverbs 17:17** - "A friend loves at all times, and a brother is born for a time of adversity" (**NIV**).This verse expresses both an obligation and a benefit. In a similar vein is the proverb that "there are friends who pretend to be friends, but there is a friend who sticks closer than a brother"

> **Proverbs 18:24** - "One who has unreliable friends soon comes to ruin, but there is a friend who sticks closer than a brother" (**NIV**).

In the Bible friendship is a mutual improvement activity, honing one for godly use. Biblical friendship is a face-to-face encounter, signifying proximity, intimate revelation and honesty. It is also a bonding of affections and trust, knitting one's very soul to another. In its ultimate reaches, it is union with God.

The Bible also warns against entering ungodly relationships.

> **Proverbs 1:10** - "My son, if sinners entice thee, consent thou not" (**KJV**).

> **Proverbs 1:15** - "My son, walk not thou in the way with them; refrain thy foot from their path" (**KJV**).

This passage and others like it caution us against the wrong types of friends but stop short of describing any type of spiritual union of souls. We also have clear warning against fornication in Scripture. "Do you not know that he who unites himself with a prostitute is one with her in body? For it is said, 'The two will become one flesh.'"

> **I Corinthians 6:16** - "What? know ye not that he which is joined to an harlot is one body? for two, saith he, shall be one flesh" **(KJV)**.

Note that the body is joined; the Bible says nothing of the souls being joined.

The Bible presents evil as addictive; however, nowhere does the Bible speak of "fragmented" souls or "dividing" one's soul. In short, the Bible gives us clear direction for our lives, and we know the remedy for sin is to confess it and forsake it:

> **I John 1:9** - "If we confess our sins, he is faithful and just to forgive us our sins, and to cleanse us from all unrighteousness" **(KJV)**.

> **John 8:11** - "She said, No man, Lord. And Jesus said unto her, Neither do I condemn thee: go, and sin no more" **(KJV)**.

There is no need for overly complex human theories such as "soul ties."

Printed in the United States
by Baker & Taylor Publisher Services